PAPERBACK
THERAPY

PAPERBACK

therapist-approved
tools and advice
for mastering your
mental health

TAMMI
MILLER
certified practising
counsellor

THERAPY

SIMON &
SCHUSTER

London · New York   Sydney · Toronto · New Delhi

PAPERBACK THERAPY
First published in Australia in 2024 by
Simon & Schuster (Australia) Pty Limited
Suite 19A, Level 1, Building C, 450 Miller Street, Cammeray, NSW 2062

10 9 8 7 6 5 4 3 2 1

Simon & Schuster: Celebrating 100 Years of Publishing in 2024.
Sydney New York London Toronto New Delhi
Visit our website at www.simonandschuster.com.au

A catalogue record for this
book is available from the
National Library of Australia

ISBN: 9781761422010

Cover design: Alissa Dinallo
Cover image: Shutterstock/gigi rosa
Typeset by Midland Typesetters, Australia
Printed and bound in Australia by Griffin Press

The paper this book is printed on is certified against the
Forest Stewardship Council® Standards. Griffin Press holds
chain of custody certification SCS-COC-001185. FSC®
promotes environmentally responsible, socially beneficial
and economically viable management of the world's forests.

Contents

Chapter 1

The therapist is in

Introduction

I am a professional therapist. I work with clients from all walks of life to help them better their wellbeing through one-on-one therapy sessions. We might work on reaching specific goals, unsticking clients from a rut, managing heavy emotions that are getting in the way of functioning day-to-day, overcoming unhelpful habits, or anything else they want to work on. Generally, though, my aim is to improve my client's self-esteem so they can take on life – and its adversities – with gusto.

I also see my own therapist for these very same things – to help me be happier. Some days my mental health is fine and I don't think I need to attend my appointment. Other days, I count down the minutes until my therapist will ask, 'What do you want to talk about today?'

When feelings interrupt our ability to function, it's always worth seeking professional support from someone who can help us find the issues that may be causing them. When we're 'in it', though, taking the step to find a mental health professional and book a therapy appointment can feel like a mountain instead of a molehill.

Maybe that's why you picked up this book – because you're feeling like life is a little too much, but you're not quite ready to make the jump into the therapist's chair. Perhaps you've been feeling low for some time and the feelgood activities you usually turn to are no longer perking you up. Or you may be experiencing a tough time due to something outside of your control – the loss of a pet or a loved one, a medical diagnosis, the end of a relationship, or stress at work. Or maybe you're just someone who is ultra-committed to their mental fitness and you see your therapist regularly, but you want to stay on top of things between sessions.

Therapy means different things to different people, and our ability to access mental health support is so dependent on our individual circumstances. There is no one-size-fits-all therapy, but the end goal is almost always the same – to improve our mental wellbeing.

Of course, it's not always possible to access the help we need. For one thing, therapy is expensive in Australia. Like, super expensive if you want to go consistently, which is what is recommended, with once a week being the ideal for maintenance. On average, the cost of a fifty-minute session in Australia starts at $100 and may cost more than $300[1] – and that's with the Australian Government's 'Better Access' Medicare rebate.[2]

I've had many a conversation with people lamenting the fact that the industry fee structure puts therapy out of reach for a lot of Australians. When questioning if it's worth seeing a therapist, we are often also questioning whether we can part with a huge chunk of our pay cheque in order to 'get results.'

That's because the general rule of thumb is that a person needs at least six sessions to see real progress, and consistency is the best way to feel supported. But we must weigh up the cost of the current state of our mental health against the cost of a therapist's fees. The result is often a decision based on the past, rather than what's needed in the present. We think, 'I've felt bad like this in the past and I eventually got over it – hopefully this time I'll just feel better soon, too,' because the thought of parting with hundreds of dollars can just be just too much to bear, especially with other rising costs of living. But just because we felt better of our own accord last time doesn't mean we will this time around. Instead of seeking qualified support as our mental health starts to suffer, we are holding on to our dollars. And it's costing us our livelihoods, and our lives.

Therapists are *absolutely* worth the money we invest. Let's be very clear about that. In Australia, training to become a counsellor takes a minimum of two years' full-time study, while a psychology degree takes a minimum of four years full-time. From there, most therapists will choose an area or areas to specialise in, such as body image disorders, mood disorders or relationship therapy, doing additional study in those areas to learn all they can for their clients. Add to that the annual clinical professional development hours, regular supervision sessions with senior peers who act as mentors and ongoing training throughout their careers, and it's clear that it takes a deep commitment to become a therapist.

The fee structure within our healthcare system in Australia, though, means that regular sessions are often too expensive for most of us. Kind of ironic that the thing that can help our anxiety can cause anxiety about money, hey?

Then there is the stigma and shame that some associate with seeing a therapist. Some people view seeing a therapist as a way to address the crises we have at a particular point in time. We're fine, until we're not, and then we're frantically asking friends and Dr Google where a 'counsellor near me' is. Others, though, see therapy as a form of main-tenance, a view we oftentimes see reflected by privileged characters in popular television series. In fact, while we used to see shame and stigma, with people who sought therapy being called 'crazy' in the pop culture of the late 1990s and early 2000s – as in *The Nanny*, *Frasier* or *Private Practice* – today's characters express pride in seeing a therapist. Just look at *Atypical* protagonist Sam and his therapist, Julia, or Connell in the screen adaptation of Sally Rooney's *Normal People*, who seeks help with his depression from his therapist, Gillian. Therapy sessions in these shows are portrayed as a source of relief, with the respective protagonists sighing deeply as they realise that someone is on their side, helping them through life's tough moments. Sam, Connell and so many other characters seeking therapy in pop culture today make it seem a lot more accessible, and even attractive.

Admittedly, Australians are better at talking about our mental health conditions now than we were ten years ago, with celebrities such as Osher Günsberg, Sarah Wilson, Melissa Leong, Jesinta and Lance 'Buddy' Franklin, Zoe Marshall, Abbie Chatfield and more publicly discussing their struggles in the media. And thank goodness they do, because the more we all realise we're not alone, the more we can come together and learn.

While discussions around mental health are increasing, actually going to *see* a therapist in Australia is still sullied by a stigma that, frankly, doesn't make sense. With an estimated one in five Australians currently experiencing some sort of mental health condition, and the need for crisis support increasing, counsellors and psychologists play a hugely important role in Australian society, and I respect them immensely. But what can you do when you can't get to the therapist's office?

You've already taken your first step towards better mental health, just by picking up this book and turning its pages. Once upon a time, I too was taking my own steps in the same direction. After decades of struggling with my mental health, I finally sought therapy and started 'doing the work'. I knew that regularly seeing a therapist would help me to regulate my emotions and better deal with adverse situations as they arose, and that it would also help me learn more about the 'why' behind those emotions.

My therapy journey had such an impact on me that I devoured psychology books to learn about why we feel the way we do, and – eventually – trained to become a therapist myself. I wanted to pass on the lessons I learned to others, to make them feel better in those moments when they felt down and out.

And that's what *Paperback Therapy* aims to do, too.

Understanding that not everyone can get to therapy, I wanted to create a book that bridges the gap between not getting any mental health support at all, and the kind of professional one-on-one support that I provide for my clients. I wanted to create the kind of book I wish I had access to when I was struggling, one that I could reference when I felt down and out, or that I could gift to my friends when they were feeling the same.

This book is not a substitute for therapy. Informed by my journey first as a client and then as a trained Certified Practising Counsellor, my goal is to provide an affordable tool to help you work through moments of poor mental health when you cannot prioritise funds for therapy, when you cannot get to an in-the-room session with a therapist, or when you're between sessions. *Paperback Therapy* aims to fight stigma by explaining how therapy works and normalising mental health fluctuations, while also making therapists' insights more accessible and affordable. It includes tips and techniques that I regularly use with my own therapy clients to help them live happier, healthier lives.

I believe that only good can come from more people having access to the tools that are shared by mental health professionals in the therapy room, and to the top-line 'how-tos' of mental wellbeing, all rooted in years of therapeutic practice. Through this book, you'll learn the basics of how therapy works, how to manage your emotions and how to have better relationships. You'll learn some of the theory behind professional counselling, as well as practical exercises that will give you the insights to better manage those tougher moments in life.

If that sounds like a lot of homework, don't worry! You can go at your own pace. I don't want you to be bogged down in the scientific language of psychotherapy. *Paperback Therapy* is purposely written in simple terms to make your mental health journey as smooth and accessible as possible. The book doesn't delve into every aspect of the profession, every mental illness, or even every facet of mental health – that would simply be too big a book to write, and everyone's therapeutic journey should be personalised to them. What the book *does* do is bring together my top tips and best advice into one digestible resource – because therapy shouldn't be overwhelming, and it should be easy to access.

How to use *Paperback Therapy*

Throughout *Paperback Therapy*, I've shared a range of my favourite easy exercises to help you work through your thoughts, feelings and behaviours. Each of these is designed to assist you to manage your mood through better emotional regulation and self-understanding.

Tools like these are designed to make you think, improve your mood in the moment, and to give you a sense of possibility. Using them regularly will help you develop your skill set (what you can do), your mindset (how you feel about what you want to do) and your tool set (the tips and techniques you can use to do it).

You can write directly onto the exercises in this book, or you can visit my website at www.baretherapy.com.au to download them for re-use over and over. This is a particularly good idea if you want to see how you grow over time (Why not try doing the Wheel of Life exercise on page 70 at the start of each new year and seeing how your circle expands?), but it can also be a great way to share what you have learned with a friend or family member who you feel could benefit from one of the exercises.

Occasionally, I'll also invite you to check in on yourself by rating your self-esteem out of ten, where a rating of 1 means 'I hate myself' and 10 means 'I love myself'. The purpose of this – as with the purpose of *Paperback Therapy* itself – is to help you identify trends in your feelings. Are certain themes within particular chapters triggering or inspiring? Do you feel better after seeing yourself reflected in some of the personal stories shared throughout the book, and realising you're not alone? For re-readers, did you feel differently about yourself the first time you read *Paperback Therapy* compared to how you feel now? What could have prompted that rise or decline in self-esteem? By identifying trends and taking a moment to look inward at how we feel about ourselves, we are taking the first step towards identifying how we can cultivate better wellbeing.

These reminders to check in with yourself will be infrequent, but they are important. They are a prompt to turn inwards and become more attuned to your feelings. Because the more we know our feelings, the more we can influence them positively.

So let's start right now.

RATE YOUR SELF-ESTEEM:

As with most things in life, you will only get out of *Paperback Therapy* what you put into it. This means getting bare, vulnerable and real with your feelings as you use this book, and it means 'doing the work' – a phrase that often comes up in this industry. To 'do the work' means to get curious about your thoughts, feelings and actions while in therapy and in between sessions. Treat *Paperback Therapy* as you would a real-life session in the room with a practising counsellor. Leave all your pretences and guards at the door as you crack its spine and sit down in your favourite armchair or comfy spot. This is a safe space, a place for you to feel heard and a place to heal.

Anything you write between the covers of this book is yours and yours alone. To ensure privacy, therapists usually code their client notes, keeping them in encrypted files or locked storage cabinets. So if it makes you feel more comfortable, find somewhere you can keep this book so you know it will be for your eyes only – maybe that's under your bed, in a box on your shelf or in a tote bag that's with you at all times. Wherever you keep it, make sure *Paperback Therapy* is easily accessible to you in those moments of need; there for you to refer to when your mind starts to wander – whether productively or unhealthily.

To get the most out of *Paperback Therapy*, I ask you to:

- Read the book with a highlighter and a pencil in hand. If something resonates and you think, 'Hey, that's just like me' or 'Hey, that's just like someone I know,' highlight it.
- Write your feelings and observations in the margins and in the 'Your thoughts' section at the back. Regularly check in and ask yourself, 'How does this make me feel?' and 'Why am I feeling this?' Use a

pencil or a different coloured pen each time you re-read, so you can see how you have grown between readings.

- Refrain from judging yourself and your feelings. All feelings are valid between these two covers. You may not know what the feeling means now, but you will in time.

- Relax. Don't worry about finishing *Paperback Therapy* all in one sitting. Your brain is plastic, not elastic. If you stop doing the work for a little while – perhaps because you feel better or have other priorities – that's okay! You won't forget everything you've learned about yourself and revert to old ways.

- Talk about *Paperback Therapy* like you talk about going to the gym, to work or to school. Think of working through the book as a part of your regular routine, a part of making you a better 'you'. Be proud of it.

- Share what you've learned from *Paperback Therapy* with your friends and loved ones. The more we talk about our mental health with others, the better for everyone.

- Head straight to the 'Seeking professional help' chapter on page 235 to access resources if you feel you need immediate crisis support.

- Get messy with this book: stain it with cathartic tears, scribble in its pages with repetitive thoughts, bend the cover and flex the spine each time you throw it in your backpack to take it to the park for a session. *Paperback Therapy* is designed to be referenced, dog-eared and worn right down – so that you don't have to be.

How does that sound? Are you ready to begin *Paperback Therapy*?

Part One

Mental Health 101

Chapter 2

Why do I feel so bad right now?

Your mental health versus the world

We can follow all the guidance and do all we can to manage our mental health, but there will come a time when we're bowled over by an outside force that throws all our good work into disarray. And it sucks when that happens – we'll think all our previous work wasn't worth it, we'll wonder 'Why me?', and the world will seem unfair.

At times like these, it's worth getting back to basics and considering Maslow's Hierarchy of Needs, the motivational theory of psychology comprising a five-tier model of human needs.[1]

At the base are *basic needs* ('Physiological needs' and 'Safety and security'), which should be met before we move up to the next level of the pyramid. The *psychological needs* ('Love and belonging' and 'Self-esteem') are the areas where our mental health can be most influenced. With these needs, the trick is to look inside of yourself to measure whether they are being met instead of leaning on others for external validation. Finally, 'Self-actualisation' is a *self-fulfilment need*, also known as a 'growth need' – in other words, it means that pursuing growth and personal development can bring about feelings of contentment, purpose, meaning and self-acceptance.

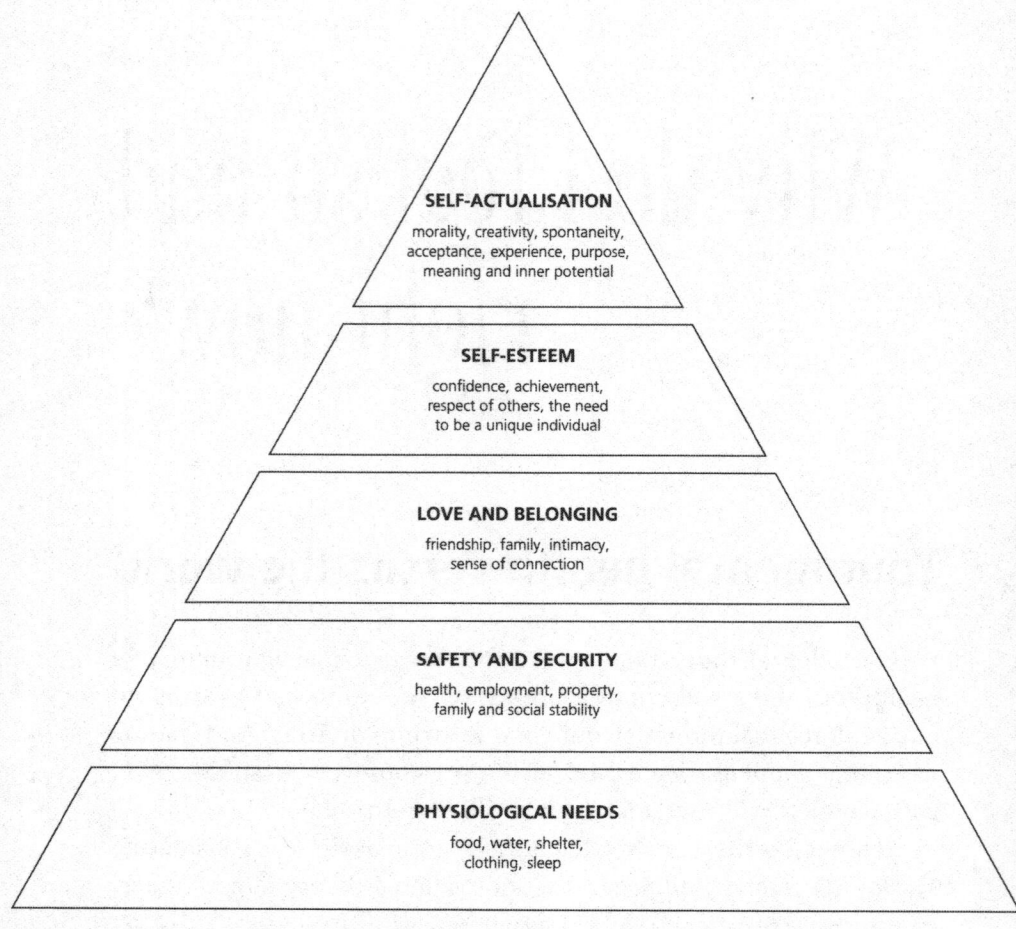

Figure 2.1 Maslow's Hierarchy of Needs.

Humans differ from other animals thanks to our imaginative drive, or hope for the future. So, while these pillars are listed as 'needs', we can also choose to look at them as motivational drivers. While Maslow once believed that the base pyramid levels had to be met before we could move on to those above, modern therapists believe there to be an overlap of needs as we climb the pyramid – for instance, some people can work on self-esteem while seeking security and safety.

By focusing our efforts too much on the pointier end of Maslow's pyramid – and jumping completely over the base levels – we can feel unstable, just like a pyramid would if we built it in the incorrect order. Essentially, unless our base-level needs are being met, we may be unable to comfortably work towards achieving the higher-tier, intangible needs.

Unfortunately, there are many outside triggers – or circumstances beyond our control – that can impact our ability to meet these basic and psychological needs. Climate change events, the cost of living crisis, global political unrest, cyberbullying, body image expectations, pandemic isolation, career comparison . . . it's understandable that we may be exhausted from swatting away the negativity that comes from things outside of our control.

Remember, though – the cards we've been dealt may be terrible, but it's important to be grateful we're still in the game.

I was in a fight-or-flight response during the pandemic, and really, the only option was to fight because I had people who relied on me in my care. Most detrimental to me personally was the fact that my output was still the same in terms of the work I had to do. Not just as an employee, but also as a wife and mother. The things that alleviated my stresses and recharged me, though, such as going out to the city for solo lunches or museum outings, long, conversation-dense catch-ups with friends, moments of quiet at beaches or on hikes – these were no longer available to me.

My family are sources of tangible support, with my mother helping with babysitting and often dropping off meals on deadline-dense days. With that support out of the picture and a partner who was an essential worker outside the home, I was stripped of the things that alleviated or reduced my stressors and enabled me the quiet, contemplative time that I needed in order to properly function.

Catherine, 38
Sydney, New South Wales

We all have to deal with circumstances beyond our control from time to time, but it's important to keep in mind that we are not alone in facing these challenges – and we can still take control even when support seems out of reach. Before we begin to look at how we can manage our external triggers, let's first consider some of the most common ones we face today.

Outside triggers

Triggers are hypothetical booby-traps that prompt an emotional response out of the blue. Some people know what their triggers are, while others aren't aware of them until a few traps catch them unawares. Feelings of unease, fear and even physical discomfort can all be brought about by an emotional trigger. Below are some of the more common ones experienced today. As you read, consider which of these triggers may be impacting your own mental wellbeing.

- **Health and wellness**: Getting the obvious one out of the way first, the COVID-19 pandemic impacted Australians (and the world) in a way none of us saw coming. Seemingly out of nowhere, our health was at risk, states were isolated from one another, and soon families and friends had to stay inside too. Outside was banned, inside was crowded, and we were robbed of that all-too-important 'third space', too: the bus ride to work or the drive to the family barbecue that helps us to self-regulate by switching off. Our most vulnerable communities suffered the most, through physical and emotional isolation, while healthcare workers worked themselves to the bone – literally, in some cases, with photos of bloody marks from face masks circulating on the internet – to keep us safe. (A huge thank you to them!) The long-term impact of the virus for some has included symptoms such as fatigue, difficulty breathing, chest pain, muscle aches, depression, anxiety and more.[2] Other effects are as yet unknown.

  And while COVID-19 continues to disrupt our lives, some of us may also be dealing with chronic health conditions. While there has been increased conversation surrounding chronic health conditions like endometriosis, heavy menstrual bleeding, diabetes, and attention-deficit/hyperactivity disorder (ADHD) – not to mention a rise in late-in-life diagnoses of the latter – it is not always easy to find specialist care and support for chronic illnesses. This can, unsurprisingly, have a big effect on our mental health. That being said, even a common cold or flu can send us into a slump!

- **School, work and career**: In 2022, 1.3 million Australians changed jobs, while 2.3 million people lost or left a job.[3] Switching up our career can influence other areas of our lives, including our overall mood. This makes sense when we consider that up to one-third of our life may be spent at work – if we're unhappy in the office, it's likely we'll be unhappy at home.

  So, why does work have such an impact? Well, there's the rationale that we need to prove ourselves in a new job (or our current one if we're worried about lay-offs or that young gun coming up the ranks), which can cause us to take on too much and to eventually burn out from overwork. There's the feeling that we need to have a career with purpose, one that helps us bring meaning to our work and give back to society. There's the changing dynamic of hybrid workplaces, which isolate us from the osmotic learning and friendships gained within the four walls of a workplace. This can also be said for being at TAFE or university, which – like work – can bring on general stress, bullying, harassment and politics, making even the best students and employees dread heading into class or work for fear of what they may encounter.

I have always been a very anxious person, since I was a child. Once I started university, the stress and anxiety became elevated. I put it down to moving away from home and having to fend for myself! When I am tired, I get very anxious and stressed. When people around me are stressed or sad it also wipes off onto me and my mood changes.

Jane, 24
Perth, Western Australia

- **The rising cost of living**: The cost of living for the average Australian has increased at an unprecedented rate over the last few years. Not only have the costs of 'big purchases' like homes and motorvehicles risen, but the everyday costs of groceries, electricity, insurance, rent, digital services and other bills have also increased. This means the stress to just get through the month financially can hang over us, increasing our mental load. In addition, it makes the bigger purchases that usually bring us joy, like holidays, seem increasingly out of reach. Without something to (realistically) look forward to and with stressful bills piling up, our mental health can suffer as we ask the existential question of 'What's the point?'

We first experience money in our families – you might hear your mum or dad talk about not having the money right now, visibly struggling to make ends meet. Or perhaps money was never spoken about because there was always enough! It's a broad spectrum of experience, and it's the first phase of us growing our own understanding of money.

From there we see what others around us have or don't have – a friend who goes on more holidays or has a nicer house, or perhaps that other friend who doesn't have money for breakfast before school. Social media plays a major role too, influencing our perspective on what's classed as 'wealthy' with potentially faked but expensive-looking feeds. We get our first jobs and start receiving pay cheques that we have to manage, and perhaps we really struggle with that! All of these things impact our understanding and behaviour with money.

**Glen James, author and host of
My Millennial Money *podcast***

- **Climate change**: According to the Climate Council, most Australians have experienced some sort of climate change disaster, such as a flood, fire, heatwave or destructive storm, in recent years.[4] When these events happen, we don't know if we will be okay, or if our friends and our families will be safe. Not only do disasters like this impact our mental health in the moment, but more than half of all Australians are worried about climate change and extreme weather events that may occur in the future.[5] For some of us, this can be a source of added anxiety.

- **Comparisonitis and life milestones**: Is your smile a little forced when your friend tells you about their new partner? Does their promotion announcement on LinkedIn have you questioning where your career is headed? Do you feel guilt when they tell you about the side hustle they worked on at the weekend, because you slept in and watched Netflix? Does the photo of them in front of a 'SOLD' sign make you feel down because you're nowhere near buying? And how about all those influencers on social media, 'living their best lives' and making you feel like yours is not enough? You're not alone. Comparisonitis, or the compulsion to compare our own accomplishments to other people's to determine how 'well' we're doing in life, is all too common in the days of social media. While we want to be happy for others, underneath it all we may be wondering when it will be our turn to reach these big, socially-agreed-upon life milestones and tick items off our bucket lists.

Then, when we do graduate from our course, buy a house, get married, buy a new car, fall pregnant, get a promotion or [insert milestone here], we fall victim to the hedonic treadmill – the psychological term for a person's tendency to never truly be happy with their success, pursuing one pleasure after another without truly feeling happy and satisfied. So I got a pay rise with my promotion? That's good, but what's next?

This is particularly difficult in moments where there is a life change that's out of our control, such as when we go from being the 'big kid' in primary school to becoming the lowest common denominator at high school, or when we go from knowing our stuff at the company we've been in for years, to having to ask the intern how to access the right SharePoint document when we become the latest hire at a new job.

Moving out of my childhood home for university in the country at seventeen years old, I gained independence quickly and focused on tertiary studies. I married young, ahead of my friends, and thought life was going well. A few years later I got divorced and threw myself into work, feeling disappointed for my failed relationship.

Living and working remotely around the world, it was a little harder for me to find a life partner and maintain social relationships. Despite travelling the globe, and achieving high levels of success in my career, in sport and in building a property portfolio, I would belittle those achievements when I saw friends announce the birth of their new babies on social media. The accomplishments I didn't yet have completely overran the ones I did, because I was comparing that one aspect of my life – having a child – with my friends and family.

Now that I have an amazing partner and a beautiful baby girl of my own, I don't know what I was so worried about. Hindsight is funny like that!

Max, 37
Lightning Ridge, New South Wales

- **Libido and sex drive**: When we're experiencing low mood or low libido, the last thing we feel like doing is getting intimate with somebody. But sex is also a stress reliever and can release happy hormones such as oxytocin – which helps with romantic attachment and feelings of love – and dopamine, the feelgood hormone that helps us pay attention, sleep and generally feel pleasure.[6] So, what to do when we're not so into it, but also know it could help?

  The pressure to have sex – whether it comes from our peers, our lovers or ourselves ('I should be having sex more regularly') – can manifest as an outside trigger, but can quickly become internalised as this cycle continues.

- **The sociopolitical landscape**: The sociopolitical context we live within can heavily impact our mental health. Components that make up our sociopolitical context might include the stability of our government, our relationships with other nations, inflation rates, unemployment levels, economic conditions, and more.

This landscape is most likely to trigger our mood if something important to us is under scrutiny or attack: for example, people of colour may feel particularly vulnerable when race is at the forefront of politics, as during the 2020 Black Lives Matter protests, or a nurse might feel anxious when a strike over wages for healthcare workers is in the headlines, and a staunch Liberal voter may feel at a loss when it looks like the Labor Party is gaining in popularity.

- **Interpersonal relationships**: Whether they originate from family, close friends or work acquaintances, the actions of other people can seriously trigger us if they are unwelcome or unexpected. These actions don't need to be intentionally directed at distressing us to trigger mood changes. For instance, your adult parents announcing their divorce may send you into a depressive spiral, you might second-guess your outfit after a stranger on the street looks you up and down, you might feel anxious after leaving a family function because your father-in-law was asking about when they would get a grandchild, or you may feel personally attacked when you overhear a colleague saying 'I hate *The Office* – it's so dumb!' because it's actually your favourite show. There's a common saying used in primary schools: 'Don't yuck somebody else's yum'. It encourages little humans to not turn their noses up or comment negatively on something their peers like. It should extend to wider humanity too – it can be very hurtful when we're saying we love something and somebody else says, 'Ew, no.'

  We can also feel bad when our interpersonal relationships come to an end, whether this is through loss of a loved one through death or a breakup, a fight with our best friend, or saying goodbye to colleagues we love when we move on to new opportunities. These changes to our social support system can impact how we see ourselves in the world, which can be hard to navigate when we're not feeling mentally strong.

- **The weather**: Yes, even the weather can be an outside trigger! Consider the last bad day you had where you couldn't quite put your finger on why you felt down. Was the sky overcast? Seasonal affective disorder (SAD) is a real depressive disorder that can take place over an entire season or just a few days.

  If we feel sluggish or irritated, have lower than usual energy, feel depressed or lose interest in activities we would otherwise enjoy –

and if we then open the windows to find the day is dreary – we may be experiencing SAD.

- **Not living according to our values**: The above list is long and non-exhaustive. But perhaps the biggest outside trigger comes when we find ourselves doing an activity that does not align with our values (see more on values in chapter 6). This could be something that happens at home (e.g. if we value 'minimalism' but the room we share with our sibling is a mess), something our friends want us to do (e.g. if we value 'lawfulness' but they want to do drugs), or something an authority like our boss or a parent wants from us (e.g. if we value 'expression' but they want us to dress in uniform or a certain way). But it can also be entirely personal, for example, if we value honesty but have recently used a white lie with a friend or employer, or if we value alone time but keep overcommitting to social events.

  Friction caused by doing something that doesn't fit with our highest values can hurt more and more over time, and eventually this outside trigger could impact our mental health.

It's okay, and even understandable, that we would be impacted in some way by items in this list. The goal is not to avoid all of these triggers, but rather to respond to them in a rational way. This can be uncomfortable at first – but like most things, we can get better with practice. Think of it like working out: our muscles and connective tissues get damaged after a tough workout at the gym, causing our body to feel sore. We may want to take a break from exercising to recover, but actually the pain is good – soreness represents our muscle fibres building back better each time, improving our strength.[7] The same happens with our minds – practice builds resilience.

As Deva and James Beck say in their 1987 book about endorphins and happiness, *The Pleasure Connection*:

> Life is filled with ongoing stressors. Stress can come in the form of changes in our job, home, or relationships. Through our response to these circumstances, we come to adapt to and settle into routine. When changes occur, we are then forced to adapt again to new situations and surroundings. Without diversity our lives could easily become boring and mundane. Change and our adaptation to change give depth, perspective and meaning to life.[8]

When life is giving us lemons, we should squeeze all the juice out of them and make lemonade. Those lemons are an opportunity – to grow, to learn, to change, to practise resilience. We can choose to question each lousy lemon that's thrown our way, asking it, 'What lesson are you offering me?' We can be changed by what happens to us, but we can also refuse to be reduced by it.

Learning what you can and cannot control

A general sense of dismay seems to infiltrate my day whenever I spend more than a few minutes on Instagram. Sometimes it's because other people's opinions are infuriating, and it reminds me of how crazy the world is; sometimes it's because I am reminded that I don't make enough money (that I can't afford nicer things or don't have a better house), or don't have the right aesthetic, or just don't have enough career success, even though on paper I am very successful and I know that what we see on socials is just part of someone's reality. It's always people's outfits, holidays, homes or careers that make me feel a bit funny.

The rational part of my brain knows it's an illusion, that they have their own issues and insecurities, but the emotional part is what takes over in that moment. I find taking little breaks or muting people really helps. It's so liberating, but I can never stay away permanently, it's too much a part of my life and work, and it can also be weirdly validating in terms of receiving likes and DMs.

Catherine, 38
Sydney, New South Wales

To harness that resilience and ensure that outside triggers flow off us like water off a duck's back, let's focus internally on what we can control. On the following page you will find a table that demonstrates how to do this, using the examples above.

OUTSIDE TRIGGER	EXAMPLE	WHAT I CAN'T CONTROL	WHAT I CAN CONTROL	THE ACTION I TAKE
Health and wellness	You get a bad case of the flu when you have a big presentation coming up	• Whether or not I have the flu – I do • The time of my presentation	• Symptom management, rest and self-care • Support from my team to step in on the presentation	• Rest • Take flu medicine • Ask my team to step in and present on my behalf
Work and career	Sunday scaries! You dread going to work because a colleague treats you poorly	• The fact that I have to work on Monday • What my colleague says to me	• How I react to my colleague • How much I let them get to me	• Deep breathe if my colleague says something nasty • Walk away from the situation • Escalate to HR if required
Rising cost of living	Your grocery shop is almost double its usual cost	• The cost of my everyday items	• What are 'needs' and what are 'wants' in my shopping trolley • The brands I buy • Discretionary spending	• Choose home-brand products instead of branded ones • Replace my afternoon takeaway latte for a tea from the office break room

OUTSIDE TRIGGER	EXAMPLE	WHAT I CAN'T CONTROL	WHAT I CAN CONTROL	THE ACTION I TAKE
Climate change	A severe storm is brewing this afternoon	• Weather patterns	• How I protect my home/myself from the storm • My insurance, if this is a regular occurrence	• Tie down any loose items outside • Set up home and contents insurance
Comparisonitis and life milestones	Yet another friend announces their engagement	• Other people's happiness • How I feel when someone gets something I want	• How I react to their announcement publicly and privately • What I say about/to them	• Congratulate my friends • Work on why I was triggered through journalling and/or therapy
Libido and sex life	It's been twenty-one days since you last had sex with your partner	• My libido, due to outside stressors	• Communication with my partner	• Talk to my partner about the situation in a respectful, open way and in a neutral place
Sociopolitical landscape	You read negative stories criticising protests for a cause you believe in	• What the media choose to write about	• How I react to the media I consume • Which media I choose to consume	• Read impartial media stories that show both sides of the story • Support my cause in other ways (e.g. donations, volunteering)

OUTSIDE TRIGGER	EXAMPLE	WHAT I CAN'T CONTROL	WHAT I CAN CONTROL	THE ACTION I TAKE
Interpersonal relationships	A friend tells you they don't like ('hate') your favourite book series	• Other people's opinions	• How other people's opinions influence my choices • How I react to other people's opinions	• Say 'agree to disagree' and move on • Choose not to take other people's opinions as a reflection on me; 'She thinks I have bad taste because I like that book' becomes 'She hates that book'
Weather	It's an overcast and grey day	• The weather	• How I mitigate negative feelings on grey days	• Use a sun lamp • Remember this is temporary – the sun will come out again
Not living according to our values	Your home is a mess, but you value 'minimalism'	• Other people's messes	• My own mess • My level of acceptance of other people's messes	• Designate an area of the home to other people (and the mess) • Set aside a day or storage in the home specifically for tidying

Exercise: Power to Control

Use the circle of control below to manage your own external triggers:

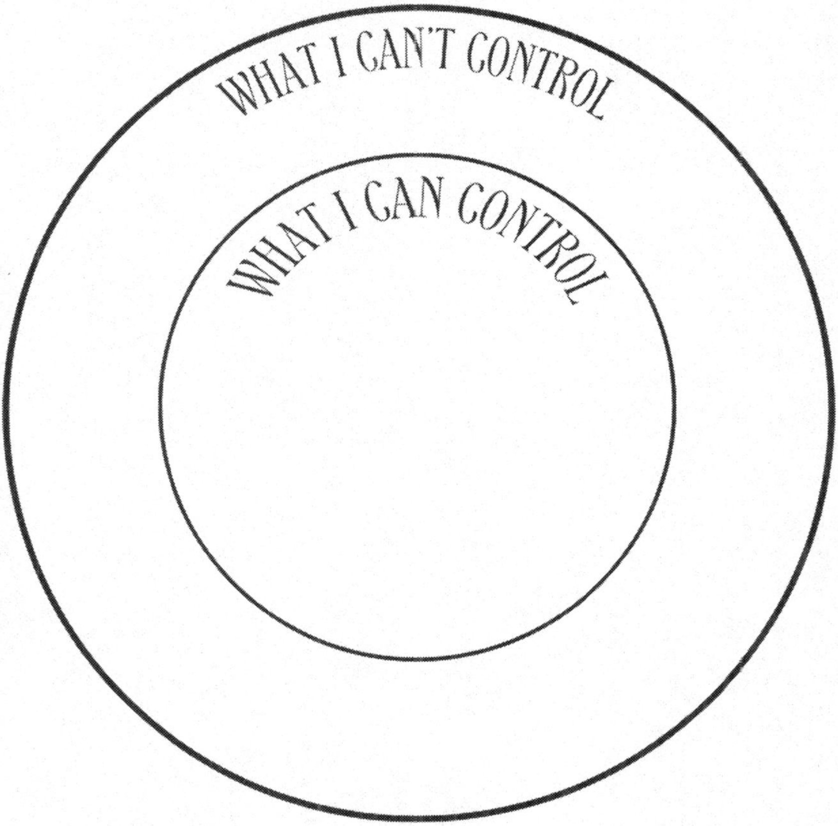

WHAT I CAN'T CONTROL

WHAT I CAN CONTROL

The key to focusing on what you can control, especially when it comes to your achievements and wants, is to make the distinction between any ambition that has personal meaning attached to it (i.e. that reflects your values and helps you live by them) and any ambition that is about proving your worth externally, to other people. Looking inside, instead of out, for validation is a task of surrender that can fill us with joy, instantly cutting away any judgements or comparisons that may make us feel bad about ourselves.

Chapter 3

Dr Google and #trending diagnoses

Why the internet might not have all the answers

If you feel like mental health is featured in every one of your feeds these days, you're not wrong. Mental health disorders and diagnoses are trending, and the jury is out as to whether this is a good or a bad thing.

The introduction of TikTok has especially increased mental health content on social media, with more people sharing their struggles and diagnoses – and providing general insight – so we can learn about the 'why' behind their feelings. Add to this Instagram, Reddit, Facebook, BeReal, YouTube and search engines, and the options for seeking mental health content online are endless.

On the one hand, it's awesome that these conditions are out in the open and being talked about in the public setting – that's the first step to reducing stigma that may be associated with mental health conditions. In addition, finding a community of people who experience life the same way we do can be incredibly validating and provide unique support in a space we naturally spend a large part of our time. We only have to look at the number of Redditors posting in various threads such as r/depression_help, r/ADHD, r/neurodiversity and r/anxiety to see that a common place to share coping skills and approaches with one another can be a good thing.

However, the other hand holds a more sinister view: that we may be self-diagnosing quite serious disorders based on unregulated information because we experience one or two similar symptoms to someone we saw online. And incorrect diagnoses can lead to ineffective treatment and can ignore the real root cause of our negative feelings.

Mental health disorders often share comorbidities, meaning those of us who experience one disorder are likely to also share symptoms of another. We may correctly self-diagnose ourselves with a first disorder (e.g. attention-deficit/hyperactivity disorder, or ADHD) but then fail to diagnose another disorder we are also experiencing (e.g. anxiety). This is why it's important to see a mental health practitioner to confirm any diagnosis, sharing all symptoms we might be struggling with instead of only those we see reflected back to us through online content.

It goes without saying that the information we find online is not always accurate. One of the most significant risks of seeking mental health advice online is that it may not be true, or it may be shared with a hidden agenda, such as by an influencer seeking followers or a brand looking to sell products.

> *Due to the social media algorithms, your feed may be overtaken with mental health content. This may unhelpfully narrow your focus of attention or sense of identity.*
>
> *I would encourage people to use information they encounter on social media as a jumping-off point, but to also see how that information fits with other sources, such as health professionals, published research and guidelines from trustworthy sources.*
>
> **Melissa Burgess, clinical psychologist**

Our anxieties may not have been invented by social media and the internet, but the digital world has given us a place to put them and multiply them, to such an extent that they can impact us daily.

Managing our social media algorithm is as much an act of self-care as any other we take towards mental wellbeing.

Prolonged social media use has been shown to expose users to mental health symptoms, with the increase in self-diagnosis being studied across the globe. For instance, a study in the journal *Comprehensive Psychiatry* looked at how people using TikTok were self-diagnosing their 'tics' as Tourette syndrome because the algorithm produced user-generated content that emotionally reinforced their beliefs.[1] In essence, when we seek out certain meanings through social media, the echo chamber of mental health content reflected back to us can actually *exacerbate* symptoms of mental disorders.

And let's not forget our old friend, comparisonitis – which can be triggered by our time spent online. Glen James, host of the *My Millennial Money* podcast, has some great advice for protecting ourselves from the perils of comparisonitis when we're online: 'Unfollow or mute any accounts on socials that lead you down a comparison footpath. Know that although it might look like your friend is living a bougie lifestyle, there's a good chance they're using debt to fund it, which means they actually can't afford it. Stay focused on your personal goals, and shoot for your personal best in everything. The best thing to do is only compare yourself to the you of yesterday and how far you have come.'

A huge positive that has come from online conversations about mental health is that long-held stigmas are slowly, slowly breaking down. There is one thing to remember, though. Navigating any content on social media is hard, and for those of us who are still figuring out how the platforms and algorithms work, it can be dangerous to blindly follow advice without the higher-level understanding that everything we see online is curated, put there with an objective in mind by the person who posts it. Questioning *why* something has been posted online while we scroll can help us maintain critical thinking.

Before there was social media, there were search engines, and with those came 'Dr Google' – the colloquial term given to the act of inputting our symptoms in the popular search engine to get a diagnosis, instead of heading to the doctor for expert advice. For some of us, searching our mental health symptoms online was an economical choice, at times when healthcare was unaffordable or inaccessible. However, the problem with digital diagnoses is that the top search results are not always likely to reflect our whole identity, and this can later impact how – and if – we seek support.

Take people of the global majority, for instance. Despite non-white peoples making up over 85 per cent of the global population, much of the mental health content online continues to be produced by white Westerners, so people from other backgrounds and cultures may struggle to see themselves represented in what they view online. And it's important to note that mental health cannot be understood in isolation from culture and identity. Advice that may work for those within one cultural, class, gender or sexual identity group may not be as well suited to those who fall outside that group.

Intersectionality is a big area for improvement. Lived experiences, whether they hinge on culture, race, gender, sexuality, class, socioeconomic backgrounds or health, massively impact on communities' willingness and ways of grappling with the complex nature of mental health.

Understanding the myriad of identity intersections that someone has allows us to wholly see them as the full human that they are. Once we acknowledge that these factors make huge differences in our lives, we can holistically and truthfully tackle mental health together.

Maggie, 24
Melbourne, Victoria

Given so much of therapy is about realising our true selves, it is beneficial to seek stories and support that represent the many facets of identity that make us *us*. For example, we may have trouble connecting with a therapist who comes from a different cultural background to our own because they don't understand that we can't simply move out of home if we're feeling stifled by our parents – in our culture, it may be the 'done thing' to care for and respect our elders. This simple example of friction that can arise in the therapeutic setting can also arise when seeking mental health support online from faceless individuals, which is why when we are looking to find out more about ourselves and our mental health struggles via a digital-first method, it's worth first seeking insight from people with similar values to our own.

Mental health as a personality trait

While it's great to have a diagnosis to better understand our mental health conditions, it can be just as important to avoid giving so much energy to our new diagnosis that it becomes a key personality trait. The term 'personality trait' itself has been co-opted by social media, with its meaning changing from 'a consistent and stable pattern of thoughts, feelings and behaviours that make up one of my characteristics' to 'something unique and all-encompassing that defines me as a person'. The difference is how much influence the trait has on us: does it contribute to a single facet of us (as in the first definition), or does it define *everything* about us (as in the second definition)?

For example, someone diagnosed with generalised anxiety disorder (GAD) may be aware that they have anxious tendencies and use strategies to manage these worries in the workplace: 'I know I have anxiety, so I'm going to write down my tasks and work through them in order of priority to mitigate my worries.' A person who views anxiety as a personality trait, however, might make the disorder a negative focal point in their lives: 'I have anxiety so I'm always going to be worrying about my to-do list and I'll never really be on top of it.' In this example, we can see how the second person is sitting wholly in their anxiety, using it as an excuse for not being on top of their to-do list. In fact, this acceptance of the disorder as a personality trait gives it a power over the person that leads them to relinquish control, which can be unhealthy and counterproductive.

It's possible to misdiagnose a mental health disorder when we're trying to do it ourselves instead of seeking confirmation from a professional. Diagnosing the wrong disorder can lead to a delay in treatment, which in turn could lead to a worsening state of mind. Seek support from a mental health professional who can diagnose using the specific diagnostic criteria developed through years and years of research, such as the Kessler Psychological Distress Scale (K10) or the *Diagnostic and Statistical Manual of Mental Disorders* (DSM).

Speaking at an ideas festival in London in 2022, journalist and high school teacher Lucy Kellaway explained the problem: 'My students have learned about anxiety through TikTok. TikTok says that if you find yourself doing this' – Kellaway fidgeted with her hair – 'or if you zone out a bit, you "have anxiety". This is making them miles worse . . . By talking about mental health without understanding anything about it, half the young people in the world have diagnosed themselves [with] a disorder, and this is really, really a problem.'

Psychotherapist and *New York Times* bestselling author Esther Perel responded: 'I'm always sensitive when we pathologise individuals instead of understanding that our society may have some troubles. The mental health crisis is a way of individualising social problems. You're not anxious. You're living exactly appropriately given the conditions of what you're going through in your life or in your family's life. That's very different.'[2]

Life can be triggering. It's full of ups and downs that we, as humans, are collectively dealing with. But there is a genuine surge of young people suffering from disorders and self-harming to cope with their symptoms. Stigma, lack of access to healthcare professionals, the inability to prioritise funds for mental healthcare and more could all be contributing to people turning online to seek information and validation about their feelings, about why they're maybe not feeling okay anymore.

The echo chamber of social media means that what people engage with is exacerbated through the algorithms. If we consume content that's all doom and gloom, we'll see more of it. Unfortunately, because of the state of the world, this isn't always avoidable. Countries are at war, financial pressure prevails, the need to be unique in a world of tall poppy syndrome is challenging, the climate is changing, and there is a myriad of other conflicts that have the potential to suck us into a 'doom and gloom' mindset online. Finding a community – any community – can help us feel less alone.

The National Youth Mental Health Survey in 2022 by headspace, Australia's non-profit youth mental health foundation, found that 58 per cent of young people feel the amount of information on social media is overwhelming. In fact, half of all young Australians felt it would be nice to disconnect from social media but worry they would miss out on things like trends, political updates or even gossip.[3] It's only human to compare ourselves to other people, and social media makes it easier to do this than ever before.

Think about it, though. Do we put our most authentic self online? Probably not. So why accept what is shared online by others as reality? We may see couples smiling and laughing together and wish we had what they have, but we don't see them doing laundry on the weekend or arguing over who does the dishes. We may feel sad seeing a story of our friend showing off their new kicks that we couldn't afford, but we may not know that their parents actually bankroll their shopping habits. Question everything, and you'll also be able to question whether your response to seeing content online is valid.

And remember, even if we don't have a diagnosis (self-diagnosed or otherwise), our feelings are still real. If we're nervous, then we're nervous. We don't need to be diagnosed with anxiety for our worries to be valid.

When celebs mind their minds

Outside of social media, mental health is discussed more and more in traditional entertainment and news media – sometimes providing distorted images that emphasise the unpredictability or dangerousness of a condition, which can impair self-esteem and prevent people seeking help.[4] Lately, though, we've been blessed with some great celebrity-informed entertainment about complex mental health that demonstrates the fact that mental health does not discriminate.

Selena Gomez's *My Mind & Me* documentary spans her six-year journey of navigating a bipolar disorder diagnosis alongside one of lupus (a chronic autoimmune disease where a person's immune system attacks their own tissues and organs). The documentary shows the singer, actress, businesswoman and philanthropist learning to live with her mental health struggles and finding purpose. She notes that despite her life looking great on the outside, she was suffering mentally and emotionally on the inside. It wasn't until Selena received a clear diagnosis that she felt understood. While she struggles with thoughts and feelings at times, she explains in the documentary that that doesn't make her faulty or weak – just human.

While stories about sports people or politicians taking a break from their careers because of mental health aren't always well received by the general public, popular culture and social media are expanding the conversation around mental health to lessen the taboo and destigmatise concepts of mental wellbeing. Films like *My Mind & Me*, and podcasts like *All in the Mind* and *The Imperfects* are part of that expanding conversation.

Australian shows like Heartbreak High *and* Please Like Me *– even* Bluey *– tackle mental health challenges openly and honestly. Independent Australian media figures such as the* Shameless *podcast hosts and Abbie Chatfield are also paving the way for a new kind of reporting, one that is values-led and unafraid of speaking up when feeling down.*

Over the past decade, the rise of social media has led to people sharing elements of their personal lives online, with mental health conditions like anxiety and depression now commonplace. The widespread normalisation of these struggles has seen people – famous or otherwise – compelled and invigorated to share their own experiences with mental health. The instantness of social media brings an element of intimacy to the mental health conversation; Instagram Stories, fleeting BeReals and off-the-cuff TikTok videos can be mediums for honest portrayals of mental health struggles.

Social media has democratised therapy in many ways – terms like 'gaslighting' and 'boundaries' have truly entered the mainstream. Its impact on the way we now speak and act upon mental health cannot be underestimated.

Maggie, 24
Melbourne, Victoria

Using social media safely

This chapter may seem like a big sign that reads 'Social media is the worst!', but it can be used safely when we log in with the right intentions. There is something to be said for finding our community, and approaching all content with curiosity will help us to do this safely. When you're next scrolling, ask yourself:

- What am I getting from this post? Does it make me feel good, or is it bringing me down?
- Why did the creator upload this content? Are they sharing their experiences, selling something, giving advice?
- Is this person an expert? How much weight should I give to what they're saying? What qualifications do they have?
- Are this person's experiences reflective of my own? Do they have the same cultural background as me? Are they of a similar age?
- Does this person follow other accounts that are also positive? Can I also follow those for wholesome content to relate to?
- Has this person said they have been diagnosed? Or do I believe them to have self-diagnosed their condition?
- Is this wholly reflective of my experience with the symptom? Or do I relate to only part of what this post says?
- Am I in the best frame of mind to be looking at this content? Am I taking it positively?

Engaging in content that educates and informs is beneficial to our mental health, but content that makes us feel worse – even if we see ourselves reflected in that content – is not helpful. Mute any accounts that make you feel worse when you see them in your feed and seek out content that improves your mood. In this way, social media may help to normalise our experiences and encourage us to seek professional help.

> I think Instagram and TikTok do such a good job in talking about mental health. It depends on your grid, but I find mine filled with quotes and inspirational stories because that's what I engage with. That being said, there is always room for improvement.
>
> **Jane, 24**
> **Perth, Western Australia**

Consider also using the tools made available to us from the platforms themselves. For instance, Pinterest has a space called 'Haven' where users can opt into seeing content that calms them or prompts them to journal their feelings. TikTok shares support resources when users search specific terms such as #suicide or #eatingdisorders.

Finally, separate influencers from professionals and put energy into listening to the latter. Follow your own therapist on social media, or click to get notifications from those who share their accreditations publicly, such as by listing any professional bodies they are members of. That way, you can be confident that the information you receive about mental health is informed and focused on making you better.

Chapter 4

CBT, DBT, ACT . . . WTF?

What is therapy?

Therapy, also known as psychotherapy, is designed to help us improve our coping skills when something external throws us for a loop. It helps to change our thought patterns and overcome any difficulties we have in understanding ourselves. Provided by a counsellor, psychologist, psychiatrist or social worker, therapy is most commonly used to manage problems relating to our mental health, though it can also be used to alter unhelpful recurring thoughts or behaviours.

Some individuals are mandated to engage in therapy following an incident, though most of us in Australia who take part in some sort of therapy do it of our own volition, with the goal of becoming better versions of ourselves.

Successful therapy can help us to:

- Manage stress, depression, anxiety, compulsions, addiction and interpersonal difficulties
- Unpack and deal with physical and mental limitations, and traumatic experiences from early life
- Navigate prejudices and inequity felt through society and culture
- Cope with loneliness, meaninglessness and existential crises

- Process grief and life transitions
- Identify and get through any recurring 'stucks' to live a better life
- Future-proof our mental health.

The main difference between therapy practitioners is the methodology they use. The table below is a guide to the three professions and is non-exhaustive.

	COUNSELLOR	PSYCHOLOGIST	PSYCHIATRIST
APPROACH	• More person-centred approach • Encourages clients to find ways to manage their own emotions through evidence-based techniques • Provides and identifies support for clients' wellbeing	• More scientific approach • Diagnoses and assesses more severe mental health problems • Encourages clients (and sometimes family/carers) to join in the decision-making process relating to treatment	• More medical approach • Diagnoses and treats more severe mental illnesses • Trained as a medical doctor and can prescribe medication as part of therapy
EXPERTS IN	• Listening and helping clients to achieve their personal goals • Short-term, solution-focused strategies	• The science of how people think, feel, behave and learn • The brain, memory, learning and processes concerning human development	• Identifying complex mental health issues • Providing a range of therapies for complex and serious mental illness

	COUNSELLOR	PSYCHOLOGIST	PSYCHIATRIST
AVERAGE LENGTH OF TERTIARY-LEVEL EDUCATION	• 3 years	• 6 years	• 11 years
REGULATION	• Self-regulated profession • Completion of accredited tertiary-level courses required to register with professional associations such as Australian Counselling Association (ACA) or Psychotherapy and Counselling Federation of Australia (PACFA)	• Regulated profession • Psychologists must be registered with the Psychology Board of Australia, which is supported by the Australian Health Practitioner Regulation Agency (AHPRA) • There are many professional associations, depending on specialty	• Regulated profession • Psychiatrists must be registered with the Australian Health Practitioner Regulation Agency (AHRPA) and must be registered with the Royal Australian & New Zealand College of Psychiatrists (RANZCP)

Note: Information correct at time of printing.

Typically, you might see a counsellor when needing some general support, and you might see a psychologist or psychiatrist for a more severe or complex mental health problem. Whether you see a counsellor, psychologist or psychiatrist, one of the keys to successful therapy is your sense of connection with your therapist. It is important to work with somebody that you feel is respectful, understanding, supportive and helpful.

Melissa Burgess, clinical psychologist

'Psychotherapy' is the umbrella term that encompasses counsellors, psychologists, psychiatrists and even social workers who use talk therapy as part of their practice when working with clients. Clients are most often individuals, though they can also include couples, families, groups and organisations.

Not a 'patient' but a 'client'

A person seeking support in therapy is most often known as a 'client' and not a 'patient'. This small nuance shifts the power dynamic back to the person seeking therapy; clients are active participants in their own mental health journeys. A 'patient' is a person receiving medical treatment, making them reliant on the medical professional. A 'client', by comparison, is a person who engages the services of another, meaning that clients are partners with their therapists, tackling their mental health together.

One of the most respected thinkers in twentieth-century psychology, American psychologist Carl Rogers, coined the term 'client-centred' therapy (later 'person-centred' therapy), which means to put the person seeking support at the centre of all that happens in the room.[1] This empowers clients with the competence to find their own solutions, *with* the help of the therapist.

Success in therapy is very often dependent on the client–therapist relationship. Established within the first session – and sometimes even within the first ten minutes – the quality of this relationship can impact how good the results (also known as therapeutic outcomes) are. This is because the counselling relationship is one based on trust and rapport, which offers us a safe space to be vulnerable and share our true emotions. The therapist then helps us to recognise and make sense of the emotions at the heart of the information we share. It's also the role of the therapist to reflect this back to us and help us to find meaning. As we can see, therapy is like a dance – the client is the lead. The closer the therapeutic relationship, the better the outcomes.

As therapy is about the person seeking support, a therapist will only disclose what is necessary about themselves for the client's benefit.

For instance, a therapist may have particular religious beliefs, attitudes or behaviours that align with our own, and choose to note this fact if they believe it will help us to feel safe and understood. However, the congruence (when the inner experience of a person matches their outward expression) will often end there. A therapist will be real, authentic and genuine with their clients but will not turn the focus of a session onto themselves. Congruence, as well as showing empathy and unconditional positive regard (accepting us completely, in a non-judgemental way, with all our strengths and weaknesses, frailties and positive traits), are tools used by therapists to build an authentic rapport with clients.

What to expect in a therapy session

A standard therapy session goes for approximately fifty minutes, with the extra ten minutes of the hour used by a therapist to manage their case notes and payments, and to prepare for their next client (not to mention allowing for a toilet break!). Most sessions are done in person in a small private room with soothing decor, comfortable chairs, water and tissues; however, many therapists also practise telehealth therapy (via online video conference), allowing clients to fit sessions into their day-to-day routines.

Each therapy session is different, though the following information will give you a good idea of what to expect.

The first session with a new therapist will differ from those that follow, and will be more of a 'get to know you' session. Therapists will use this time to understand our reasons for seeking help (known as our 'presenting problem'), our history and closest inter-personal relationships, and any information that may be pertinent to our presenting problem/s. We'll disclose this information during the initial 'intake,' and it may appear our therapist is asking standard questions that don't have too much to do with our reason for attending therapy. What they are doing is forming a full picture of us so they can help us to identify any trends. This information gathering is known as a 'case formulation.'

Before starting this intake session, our therapist will inform us of what to expect in the session and their duty as a mandatory reporter. For example, they might say something like:

A typical therapy session with me entails [x, y and z]. This is a safe space for you to be vulnerable. You have the right to ask any questions about my therapy process, and about my qualifications and experience. Everything you say in this session will remain confidential to me; however, there are exceptions to that rule. For instance, if you sign a document that says I can share information with other support people in your wider health-care team [such as a GP or psychiatrist], then that form allows me to break confidentiality. Alternatively, if I identify that you are a risk to yourself or another person, such as by suicide or abuse or neglect, I am mandated [by a professional organisation/my ethical code of conduct] to inform other people such as the authorities – we need to keep you safe and we need to keep others safe. Finally, if a judge subpoenas your records for court, I must hand them over. How does that sound? Do you have any questions?

This is usually explained verbally, though it can also involve a therapist sharing a form for us to sign that details the services we will receive, how we agree to conduct ourselves in therapy (openly, respectfully, honestly), appointment and fee structures, any insurance or rebates, confidential record keeping, the therapist's availability and contact details, and any other rights we have as clients.

In doing the above, the therapist is asking for our informed consent to move ahead with therapy – meaning we are aware of our rights as clients and consent to continuing the therapeutic relationship.

Therapy isn't about what the therapist gets from us, but what we get from the therapist. For the first session, this involves building a rapport with one another. The therapist should present to us with unconditional positive regard, whereby we as clients are accepted and supported no matter what we say or do (outside of being abusive, of course). This will enable the best therapeutic results, and if something feels 'off' between a client and a therapist following the first session, as clients we have the right to ask ourselves whether we're just uncomfortable because we were vulnerable where we hadn't previously been, or whether maybe this isn't the therapist for us (that's okay – see chapter 17 on 'Seeking professional help' for tips on how to find the right one).

———

Once we've gotten into a rhythm with our therapist, they'll work with us to identify the biggest hurdles that we wish to overcome in our sessions – and the strategies to help us do so. These hurdles might be the presenting problem/s we first booked a therapy appointment for (trouble sleeping, feeling lonely, increased anger, etc.), or they may be larger issues that manifest in those symptoms (bullying, neglect, low self-esteem, etc.). Our therapist will call upon their professional experience and preferred types of therapy (see later in this chapter) to work with us towards better wellbeing.

To ensure we get the most out of therapy, the therapist may ask us:

- If we would like to do 'homework' between sessions, or if we would prefer to work in the room only
- If we tend to routinely take a task and run with it, or if it's a little harder for us to get started
- If we're going about this journey alone or if we have a support system of friends and/or family around us.

All of this is to help them understand us, and ensure we're working together in a way that will make us feel better in the long term.

Our therapist may also check in to find out if we feel we're getting what we need from therapy. This isn't about them, but rather to ensure that we feel *understood* and *supported*. Stripping away everything else, that's really all therapy is.

———

Later in our therapy sessions, after several weeks or months, we may find ourselves without anything pertinent to say. In these moments, a therapist may want to hear more about something trivial discussed in a previous session. That's because they believe there to be a reason we brought it up, and want us to explore this more. That's when the underlying topic may emerge.

As psychotherapist Lori Gottlieb writes in her *New York Times* bestseller *Maybe You Should Talk to Someone*: 'It takes a while to hear a person's story and for that person to tell it, and like most stories – including mine – it bounces all over the place before you know what the plot really is.'[2]

By holding space for us – through nodding, asking us to continue, reflecting and summarising back to us what we've told them – a therapist can help us to get to the core of a new topic we may wish to explore.

Mental health disorders and diagnoses

The terminology used in therapy is important, but it can get confusing. For instance, here is the difference between mental health, wellbeing, illness and disorder, as it is currently understood in the industry:

- **Mental health**: Our emotional, psychological, and social wellbeing. Everyone has mental health; however, the degree of its stability and positivity can differ from person to person, from day to day and even from hour to hour. When our mental health hits – or drops below – a certain threshold, we may seek therapy.
- **Mental wellbeing**: A positive state of mental health, whereby we can cope, learn, work and engage with life well.
- **Mental illness**: Complex mental health challenges that aren't just part of daily life. More chronic in nature, a mental illness is diagnosed through the use of a clinical tool that determines whether symptoms meet a standard set of criteria (see below).
- **Mental disorder**: Often used interchangeably with 'mental illness', mental disorders are a subset based on the clinically significant symptoms we have. For instance, we may have an 'anxiety disorder', an 'eating disorder' or a 'neurodevelopmental disorder'.

We all have *mental health*. We can all target *mental wellbeing*.

We don't need to have a clinically significant mental illness or disorder to seek therapy. In fact, many clients see their therapist to better their mental wellbeing through strategies they can implement every day. When those strategies no longer work, though, clinical checklists and questionnaires - such as the Kessler Psychological Distress Scale (K10) or the *Diagnostic and Statistical Manual of Mental Disorders* (DSM) - can help with making a diagnosis.

When used by trained professionals, these tools can help us better understand our mental health, as often happens when we are diagnosed. It's always best to see a professional for a formal diagnosis, rather than self-diagnosing by matching our symptoms to those we may see online, as a correct diagnosis and a mental healthcare plan that matches our needs will lead to better mental wellbeing sooner.

The stigma associated with going to therapy

By now, we've learned that therapists are well-trained professionals in the field of mental health whose number one priority is improving their clients' wellbeing. They are people who can be in our corner, people we can talk to confidentially, people who will hear us without judgement when we are at our most vulnerable. Sounds pretty helpful, right? So why is there still a stigma associated with going to therapy?[3]

In the past, this shame existed because of a lack of understanding about what therapy actually is. Back when social media was just a figment of Mark Zuckerberg's imagination, many people believed that we only seek therapy when we're in the thick of a mental health crisis. And talking about our mental health crisis with friends and family? Well, that just wasn't done. So, we would make excuses to get out of class or work early ('I have a doctor's appointment', 'I've got to pick the kids up from school') or take our desk lunch alfresco for once, to head to our fifty-minute therapy session in secret.

Only when celebrities, influencers and the people around us started talking about mental health via traditional and social media did this shame start to erode. In the early years of the COVID-19 pandemic, the

Australian Government recognised the importance of therapy during self-isolation, and increased the number of therapy sessions we could access via Medicare from ten to twenty per calendar year (though this was later reversed).[4] Now, with more talk in the media about mental health, we're well on our way to having the shame associated with going to therapy relegated to the history books.

However, there is still a great deal of work to be done. Aboriginal and Torres Strait Islander people, members of the LGBTQIA+ community, and culturally and linguistically diverse (CALD) communities can experience discrimination from society with regards to mental illness, causing even greater impacts on mental health, and thus perpetuating a cycle of stigma and shame. Specialist mental health practitioners are trained from and for engagement with these communities – but that doesn't mean that everyone has the means to access therapy. See page 244 for some specific support available to these communities.

Our mental health doesn't need to be a battle – though on some days it might seem like just that. We can work on our mental wellbeing every day. Let's not wait until we're in the midst of a crisis. Recognise therapy for what it is: a proactive tool for contentment in life.

> *I am proud to be seeing a therapist because, to me, it is no different to seeing a dentist for a sore tooth or a physio for a sore back. Our brain is a major organ, and it needs some love and care! A lot of my friends do see a therapist, and we share with each other how our sessions go.*
>
> **Jane, 24**
> **Perth, Western Australia**

The client–therapist relationship

The relationship we have with our therapist is one built on trust. If we feel understood and heard when in the room, the therapist is halfway there. Often, though, the feelings brought up in the therapy room can be confusing – for one or both of you.

Transference and countertransference are discussed often in a mental health practitioner's training. Transference is when a client redirects their feelings for another person onto their therapist (e.g. we might see a therapist as a father figure because they have similar qualities to our dad). Countertransference is the reverse, when a therapist redirects their own desires or feelings onto their clients (e.g. they may find themselves thinking about going to coffee with us because they like us). While transference and countertransference can sometimes be a normal and even useful part of the therapeutic process, therapists are trained to identify and course-correct any instances that blur the boundaries of professionalism and ethics. Diving into *why* these feelings have occurred in the first place can give a therapist greater insight into the client and their needs.

It is key to remember that a therapist is just a person. Therapists are not oracles or magicians or knowers of all things. They don't have all the answers but, because they have our best interests at heart, they will do their best to help us find them. If they're ever unsure of the way forward or the answer to a question we ask, they will say 'I don't know' and work on getting us some feedback the next week. Being authentic while in session goes both ways.

It's challenging to feel safe in a space and with a therapist that you don't align with. What is important to them as a value set varies from person to person, but I view finding a therapist much like dating; you are not always going to gel with everyone you 'date' and it takes time to find the therapist that has a synergy with your background and needs. For me, it was imperative my therapist had experience with CALD communities, was trauma informed, and also didn't bring their bias/personal views to our sessions (which I have experienced).

Hawraa, 30
Melbourne, Victoria

And even therapists need therapists! Good therapists seek mentorship from senior peers, go to therapy themselves, and engage in continuing professional development to ensure their skills and knowledge are up to date with the latest research.

Common therapy styles

The first inklings of therapy were thought to come from Ancient Greece, where philosophers Plato and Aristotle, and physician Hippocrates examined mental health alongside medicine. The exact moment that therapy as we know it today was born is difficult to pinpoint. For hundreds of years, people have sought one-on-one conversations to better understand stresses in their lives, interpersonal relationships, doubts or fears they may have, emotional challenges and mental health disorders. At which point did those conversations become professionally influenced and skew towards psychotherapy?

Several physicians focusing on hypnosis and dreams during the 1800s receive credit in the history books for early psychotherapy, most of them dispelling the commonly held belief of the time that mental illness was associated with witchcraft and other supernatural forces. Psychotherapy as we know it – 'talk therapy' – didn't truly explode until the late 1800s when Josef Breuer's 'talking cure for nervous disorders' was explored by Breuer and his medical colleague Sigmund Freud. Many of Freud's students would expand upon his work, deepening the field of psychoanalysis and evolving psychodynamic therapy.

Since then, across the various psychotherapy fields of psychiatry, psychology, counselling and more, the industry has grown alongside our search for meaning. While some experimental research conducted by therapists in previous years was questionable (Google 'Stanford prison experiment' or 'Little Albert experiment'), all roads lead to today – a growing, much more ethical field with one common goal in mind: to better understand human behaviour and help clients in therapy to live happier, healthier and more productive lives.

———

There are so many styles of therapy a practitioner can choose to specialise in, and through the years those styles gave way to others, and others again, each backed by research and observations, and each with different techniques and strategies that could be used in the room. With many facets of therapy using scientific terminology that is not often shared beyond those who work in the field, it's understandable that we might hear 'CBT' and 'DBT' and 'ACT' and think, 'WTF? I just want some help!'

Health literacy means having the knowledge and motivation to understand, judge and apply information to make effective decisions about your own health and healthcare options. Health literacy is also the reason for this chapter, which will give you a basic understanding of modern psychotherapy so that when you search for a therapist or speak with one for the first time, you can listen, learn and make informed decisions about your next steps.

Therapy modalities tend to fall into the following schools:

- **Psychodynamic**: Psychodynamic approaches focus on the unconscious influences on the way we function. We would talk at length about issues on our mind, aiming to uncover common thoughts or behaviours that may be causing discomfort and improve our ability to exercise greater conscious control over them.
- **Humanistic-existential**: Based on the belief that we have the best understanding of our own unique experiences and needs, humanistic-existential therapy focuses on improving human potential. Those who practise this style of therapy believe that the client has the best understanding of their own unique experiences and needs, and has the capacity to choose how we exist in the world.
- **Cognitive behavioural**: The way we think and how we behave when identifying and addressing our problems is central to the cognitive behavioural school of therapy. Therapists will assess clients, then intervene to help change specific behaviours or thoughts. This is a much briefer approach than psychodynamic and humanistic-existential therapies.

- **Postmodern**: Working from the view that the way we construct and process information about ourselves and our world is central to our identity, postmodern modalities pull from the past to inform the present.

The style of therapy a practitioner chooses to use in the room depends on their training or specialty, and on their clients' unique needs. For instance, even though someone may have specialised in cognitive behavioural therapy (CBT), if a client presents each week to therapy with low self-esteem and continues saying 'I am so unlovable. No one will ever love me', the therapist may want to try something new.

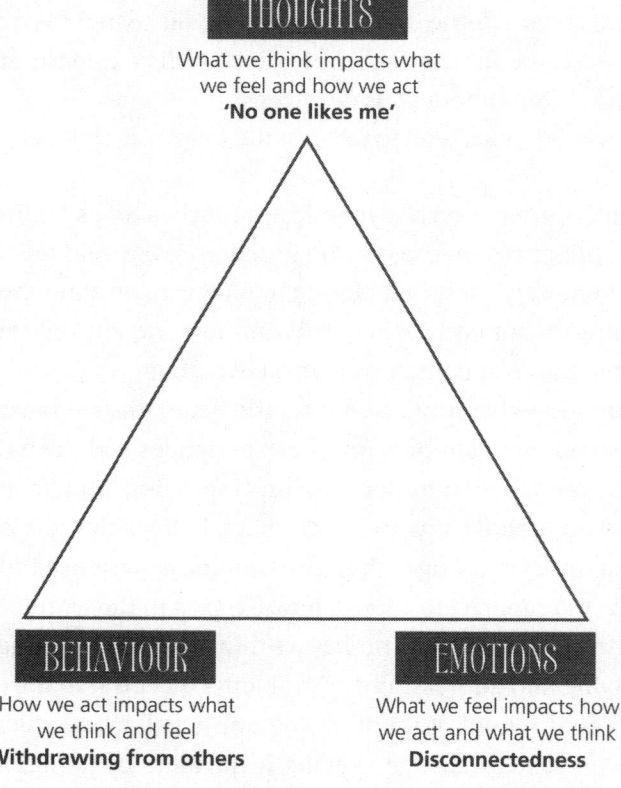

Figure 4.1 The cognitive triangle, commonly used in the cognitive behavioural modalities to demonstrate how our thoughts, emotions and behaviour are interconnected.

Perhaps the therapist remembers that the client described themselves as 'creative' in the first session, and has seen a journal poking out of their bag each time they're on the couch, so at the next session the therapist brings some coloured pencils to practise art therapy techniques to come at the problem another way. The therapist might ask the client to draw themselves on the page, and then guide them gently to add in 'one person who has called you nice', 'your pet', 'one person who you can call when you feel down', 'the colleague who bought you a coffee', and so on. By drawing each of these onto the page, the client can see that, actually, they are surrounded by people who love them, and so the absolutist thinking of 'I am unlovable' is actually a false thought.

> I first came across CBT when doing therapy for an eating disorder. It was good for me to talk to someone for an hour, but I needed strategies to use for the other twenty-three hours of the day, and that's where CBT really helped me to manage my anxieties. I had different techniques, tools and mantras to use for different iterations of my anxiety, in a very practical way. For me, the visual reminder of tools and goals that helped me to change also helped me to see how far I had come. Sometimes you think you haven't come very far, and then you see all those goals ticked off and it feels really good.
>
> **Nadine, 40**
> **Sydney, New South Wales**

Most therapists don't commit to using just one therapeutic approach. Instead, they blend elements from many to best suit the requirements in session. This is called an integrated or holistic approach, and is person-centred in that it puts our needs at the heart of the work.

Because of clinical research and studies into the success of all kinds of therapeutic strategies on various presenting problems throughout the years, there is no shortage of ways a therapist can work with us. For instance, we may want tangible strategies we can put into play between sessions (like homework) because we believe every problem has a solution. Psychodynamic talk therapy may not suit this kind of personality, and so our therapist may choose CBT so we can clearly see 'what we're supposed to do' in order to see progress towards our goals.

Some common therapeutic modalities and common issues they are used for are listed below.

ACCEPTANCE AND COMMITMENT THERAPY (ACT)	**Good for**: Anxiety, depression, work stress, chronic pain, eating disorders, obsessive-compulsive disorders, substance use disorders, etc. **School**: Cognitive behavioural
ANALYTICAL THERAPY	**Good for**: Inner suffering, self-awareness, anxiety, depression, eating disorders, phobias, etc. **School**: Psychodynamic
BEHAVIOUR THERAPY	**Good for**: Depression, anxiety, panic disorders, anger, etc. **School**: Cognitive behavioural
COGNITIVE THERAPY	**Good for:** Anxiety, self-esteem, substance use disorders, bipolar disorder, phobias, eating disorders, etc. **School**: Cognitive behavioural
COGNITIVE BEHAVIOURAL THERAPY	**Good for**: Depression, anxiety, bipolar disorder, eating disorders, post-traumatic stress disorder, obsessive-compulsive disorders, phobias, etc. **School**: Cognitive behavioural
CREATIVE THERAPIES (ART, DANCE, DRAMA, EXPRESSIVE ARTS, MUSIC, PLAY)	**Good for**: Anxiety, trauma, depression, post-traumatic stress disorder, eating disorders, etc. **School**: Postmodern
DIALECTICAL BEHAVIOUR THERAPY (DBT)	**Good for**: Personality disorders, eating disorders, self-harm, post-traumatic stress disorder, depression, anxiety, substance use disorders, bipolar disorder, etc. **School**: Cognitive behavioural
EXISTENTIAL THERAPY	**Good for:** Anxiety, substance use disorders, depression, etc. **School**: Humanistic-existential

GESTALT THERAPY	**Good for**: Self-esteem, anxiety, depression, bipolar disorder, interpersonal relationships, chronic pain, etc.
	School: Humanistic-existential
GROUP AND FAMILY THERAPY	**Good for**: Family and other interpersonal conflict, depression, anxiety, substance use disorders, bipolar disorder, personality disorders, eating disorders, coping with chronic medical issues, etc.
	School: Humanistic-existential
MULTIMODAL THERAPY	**Good for**: Depression, anxiety, personality disorders, substance use disorders, eating disorders, brain injuries, etc.
	School: Cognitive behavioural
NARRATIVE THERAPY	**Good for**: Anxiety, trauma, substance use disorders, eating disorders, anger, depression, etc.
	School: Postmodern
PERSON-CENTRED THERAPY	**Good for**: Anxiety, depression, grief, abuse, life changes, interpersonal conflict, etc.
	School: Humanistic-existential
POSITIVE THERAPY	**Good for**: Depression, anxiety, self-esteem, etc.
	School: Postmodern
PSYCHOANALYSIS (CLASSICAL)	**Good for:** Anxiety, personality disorders, phobias, sexual problems, depression, etc.
	School: Psychodynamic
RATIONAL EMOTIVE BEHAVIOUR THERAPY	**Good for**: Anxiety, depression, self-worth, anger, procrastination, eating disorders, etc.
	School: Cognitive behavioural
SCHEMA THERAPY	**Good for**: Borderline personality disorder, eating disorders, anxiety, depression, etc.
	School: Cognitive behavioural
SOLUTION-FOCUSED BRIEF THERAPY (SFBT)	**Good for:** Substance use disorders, interpersonal relationships, anxiety, depression, gambling addiction, eating disorders, etc.
	School: Postmodern
TRANSACTIONAL ANALYSIS	**Good for:** Self-esteem, interpersonal relationships, anxiety, etc.
	School: Humanistic-existential

> DBT has changed my life; I use every skill daily and all the time to assist with my BPD [bipolar disorder] and mental health. Without it, I wouldn't be here. Some of my favourite skills are Opposite Actions and Wise Mind.
>
> **Ashira, 26**
> **Melbourne, Victoria**

Luckily, we don't need to know exactly what style of therapy is right for us before seeking professional help. In fact, most therapists would prefer we reach out and enquire about their services by sharing the issues we are looking to work on, instead of dictating the style we wish them to use. If they don't feel they can help us, they'll direct us to someone who can. And remember, often the rapport we have with our therapist will be the best indicator of success.

Part Two

Your Guide to Mental Wellbeing

Chapter 5

Get ready to change your life

Goal setting and the stages of change

By simply reading this book, you are actively engaged in changing your life for the better.

We are all in different situations. You may be considering changing your behaviour in the coming months but not just yet. You may be taking the first step right now, or you may even be actively working towards your goals already. These are all different stages of readiness to change, of which there are six in total. The stage you are in determines how likely you are to stick with changed behaviours, and how long it may take you to reach your goals.

Stages of readiness to change

No matter whether our goal is to change how much we binge eat, how often we say 'yes' to drugs or drinking excessively, how we cower when someone calls on us to make a presentation, how we say 'yes' when we really mean 'no', or any another behaviour that is holding us back, we're somewhere within the six stages of readiness to change. The six stages model is commonly used for substance use rehabilitation, though it can be applied for most behaviours that require adjustment. It's important to note, too, that in order to change our behaviour, we may need to filter through the stages of readiness to change a number of times. That is okay. The key is just to keep moving forward.

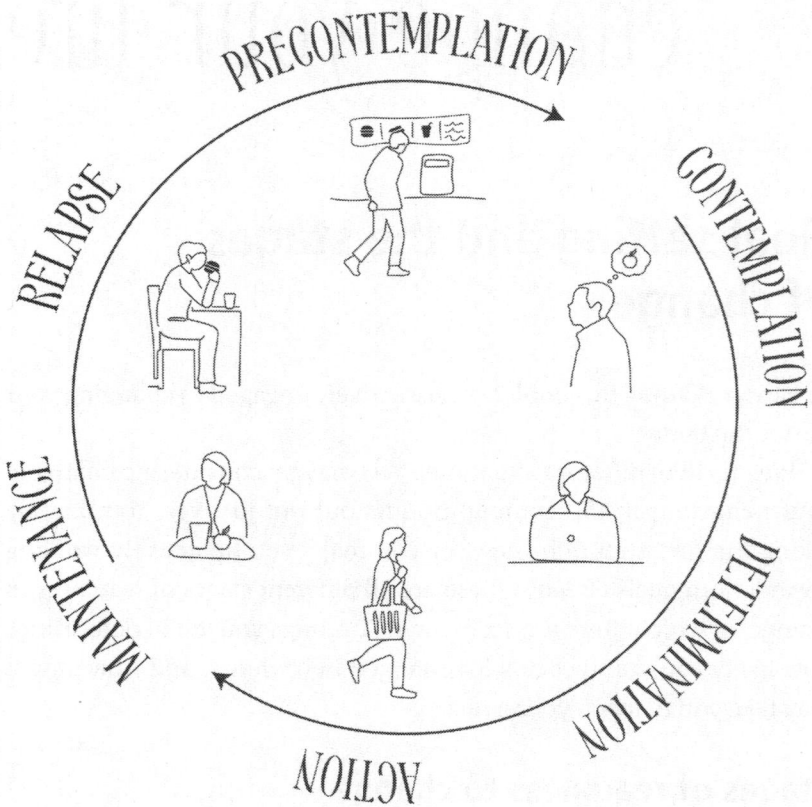

Figure 5.1 Six stages of readiness to change. The example is someone changing the behaviour of eating unhealthily to eating healthily.

1. **Precontemplation**: In this stage, we do not yet acknowledge there is a problem and actually may be in denial about our issue. We are not thinking seriously about change and any attempt from external parties to help us change while we're in this stage will be met with defensiveness. In this stage, we often don't believe we have a problem that needs changing at all.

2. **Contemplation**: We are aware there is a problem but are not yet ready or confident enough to make a change. If we're in this stage, we're likely big fans of the 'pros and cons' list, weighing up the benefits of changing against the negative aspects of our habit. We may feel that the long-term benefits don't yet outweigh the short-term costs.

3. **Determination**: Now we are committed to changing and aware of the seriousness of our negative behaviour. This is the optimum moment to ask for help – or to help someone else who may be in this stage – as we are likely researching the support we can seek, how we can change our behaviour and how the change is going to impact our lifestyle. The latter is important research and should not be skipped, as jumping straight from Contemplation to Action can increase risk of relapse because of the shock of change.

4. **Action**: In this stage, we actively take the steps to change our behaviour. Our willpower is strong, and alongside our action, we make plans to manage any relapses caused by internal or external pressures. We talk to close friends, family and/or our therapist to seek support on our journey. Usually, a person in the action stage will use short-term rewards to maintain motivation, such as a star chart or a dinner out to celebrate reaching the first milestone. While this stage is a very important one, a single slip-up can often lead to immediate relapse and starting the journey all over again. Acknowledging our misstep and getting back on track immediately will help us move on to the next stage sooner.

5. **Maintenance**: Anyone who has successfully taken steps to change their behaviour wants to stay in the Maintenance stage as long as possible. Here, we are successfully avoiding external pressures and temptations, and we have visual or written cues nearby that

remind us of how far we have come. We are very aware of what might trigger relapse, and know what to do should those triggers occur. We are also self-aware, acknowledging how far we have come and that it takes work (constant check-ins, therapy, social support, mindfulness exercises, group work, etc.) to stay on our new path.

6. **Relapse**: Resuming old behaviours and abandoning all changes is called relapsing, and it is linked very closely with Precontemplation. There is often a lot of guilt and negative self-talk when we hit this stage, especially if we were in the Maintenance stage for a long time. This can lead to relapsing further ('I've broken my habits now – one more time won't matter'). However, that's why Relapse is included in the stages of change: to reframe it as a common and natural part of the change process, rather than as a 'failure'. The key when entering relapse is to identify the triggers that caused it to happen, and to make a plan to avoid those triggers in future. This could mean speaking with our support people, and reaffirming our commitment to changing our behaviour. By doing this, we can skip through sitting in the Precontemplation stage again, instead heading straight for Contemplation – and plans for Action.

―――――

Sometimes when we're in the thick of a negative behaviour or habit, it's hard to identify that we really do want to change it. This is especially the case if our peers are also partaking in that behaviour (for example, if we binge drink with our friends) and they aren't in the same stage of readiness to change as we are. This is where therapists can support us to identify more strongly with our commitment to change, and to manage any external triggers (like when our friends pressure us to have 'just one beer'), should they arise.

Exercise: Stages of Change

Can you identify which stage you are in right now? Write below the behaviour you're looking to change, and the stage you are in.

BEHAVIOUR TO CHANGE	STAGE I'M IN NOW	DATE
Stop biting my nails *(Because it looks yucky and isn't a healthy way to cope with my anxiety)*	*Contemplation* *(I know I need to break this habit, but I'm about to enter exams and so know I won't be successful now)*	*23.03.2024*

As you work your way through *Paperback Therapy*, the stage you're in might change – mostly forward, but sometimes backward. Make note of those changes in the table above, and remember that two steps forward and one step back is still one step forward.

In my age group, I feel like females are more on top of being comfortable with talking about mental health compared to males. It's kind of becoming trendy to talk about it, and to express how you feel. I do worry for my male friends, but the stigma has definitely lessened over the last few years.

Jane, 24
Perth, Western Australia

A therapist can't convince us to go to therapy, to stop drinking, to quit drugs, to switch careers . . . but what they can do is ask us the right questions that will lead us towards Contemplation and Action, using a technique called *motivational interviewing*.

The key purpose of the motivational interviewing technique is to help us identify the discrepancy between our goals and our values, and our current (problematic) behaviour. It's about identifying the incongruities between what we want and where we are. When it becomes clearly obvious that what we're currently doing is not helping us reach our goals, we're more likely to change.

So, let's get into the habit of asking ourselves: 'Does this support the life I'm hoping to create?' If the answer is no, it's time to change our behaviour.

Setting goals for better mental health

Let's get clear about what kind of life it is you're trying to create. Goals can help us focus and get momentum in life, allowing us to grow and achieve. When we tick something off our list of goals (no matter how big or small), we get a little hit of dopamine (the happiness hormone in our brains) – that's why it feels good to get through your to-do list!

Exercise: Goal Setting

Sometimes it is easy to set goals but difficult to know how to reach them. The table below will help you to break your bigger goals in life down into little actionable tasks.

Try writing your goals 'SMART'-ly so you can easily measure when you've reached them, and improve upon them next time you set a similar one:

- **S**pecific: What do I want to accomplish? e.g. 'I want to save money'.
- **M**easurable: How will I tell when it has been accomplished? e.g. 'When I have $5000 in my savings account'.
- **A**chievable: Is this actually something I can accomplish, and how? e.g. 'Yes, I earn enough that I could put some money away each pay cheque and reach my goal'.
- **R**elevant: Is this goal worthwhile? e.g. 'Yes, because then I can go on that holiday with my friend'.
- **T**ime-based: When should I aim to achieve this? e.g. 'I want to save $5000 by 1 December for the holiday at the end of January'.

The above would be written in the 'My Goal' column of this exercise as: 'To save $5000 by 1 December to pay for my holiday in January'.

As you complete each goal, you will be one step closer to a happier, healthier you.

	MY GOAL	WHAT I'M DOING WELL
FRIENDS		
FAMILY		
WORK		
SPIRITUALITY		
STUDY		
MIND		
BODY		
OTHER		

WHAT I COULD IMPROVE ON	A SMALL CHANGE I CAN MAKE TOWARDS MY GOAL TODAY

If we're looking to change our current behaviour, it's likely because it is causing negative personal, emotional, relational or social impacts. In fact, it may be taking us further away from our goal and that's why we're feeling ill at ease.

However, verbalising the incongruence between what we want from life and where we are is a lot different than simply being aware of it. That's where the 'On the One Hand' technique comes in. Demonstrating discrepancies is easily done through this technique, in which we frame ourselves a 'this or that' question, for example, '*On the one hand*, I want to live long enough to see my grandkids graduate. But *on the other hand*, I'm not monitoring my sugar levels to manage my diabetes. How will that help me live long enough to see my grandkids graduate?'

Using this technique can make it obvious to us that change is needed and so move us through to the next stage.

It can be hard to manage our negative moods if we aren't in a Contemplation or Determination stage of change, which is why a technique like motivational interviewing is important – it is designed to demonstrate these discrepancies and help us reflect on those negative moods.

However, if we're not yet in therapy, how can we make use of those techniques to help move towards our end goal?

Never underestimate the power of the 'pros and cons' list – a self-directed 'On the One Hand' exercise on the following page. We can use it to consider whether it's worth going to therapy.

> *Therapy is helpful for anybody, and you don't need a big reason to justify going. If you don't like how you feel, if you are feeling stuck, if you are feeling overwhelmed, or if you are just interested in therapy, you should give it a go. The only 'wrong' reason to do therapy is when you are doing it because other people want you to, and you aren't genuinely interested. If you aren't open to trying therapy, it is unlikely to work.*
>
> **Melissa Burgess, clinical psychologist**

GOING TO THERAPY	
PROS	**CONS**
• I will learn strategies to make me feel better	• I'll need to be vulnerable with a stranger
• It might help me find ways to stop self-sabotaging	• It might be expensive
• I can do it without anyone but me and the therapist knowing	• It might retraumatise me
• I can talk to someone neutral about my interpersonal relationships	• My friends might think I'm 'crazy'
• I can finally work on that stuff that happened when I was younger	• It requires a regular time commitment
• It will help me understand why I feel the way I do	• It will be hard and uncomfortable
• It will help me better understand what I want out of life	• I might not like my therapist or they might not like me
• I'll get advice and guidance from an expert instead of my friends/family	
• It will get easier as I go along	

Exercise: Pros and Cons

Use the below 'pros and cons' list on a change you're consider-ing making but you might be a little ambivalent about. By identifying more, or stronger, pros on your list, you're more likely to commit and adhere to a plan towards change.

I want to change...

PROS	CONS

Taking a moment to reflect

Sometimes we don't know exactly what we need to change – we just know that something has to. For instance, we might feel like we're in a 'rut' but not know how to take the first step towards digging ourselves out of it. In these instances, reflective prompts can identify deep-seated desires for change. Then we can change our behaviour to focus our attention where it's needed, as identified in the Wheel of Life exercise (see page 70).

Exercise: Reflective Prompts

These prompts can help you to identify if and what you wish to change, while also driving self-efficacy by bringing to the fore your support systems, capabilities and immediate actions you can take to better your mental wellbeing. Use the notes section at the back of *Paperback Therapy* to answer these prompts:

- What thoughts continue to pop into your head? Are they nourishing or intrusive?
- What's one action you can take now, to improve your self-esteem?
- What is something you love about yourself?
- What did you learn about yourself today?
- What do you want to accomplish in the next 365 days?
- Who is someone you are grateful for?
- What would you tell yourself 5 years ago?
- What continues to take your attention? Is it something you value?
- What sensations can you feel in your body today?
- Who helps you to be the best version of you, and why?
- How can you regulate your emotions today?
- What have you done to play today?
- What is something you are grateful for?
- What spiritual needs can you nourish today?
- What emotional needs can you nourish today?
- What physical needs can you nourish today?
- What are three things you are good at?
- If you were to completely give in to life and live it fully, what's the first change you would make?
- What achievements are you most proud of?
- What are three things that would make a big difference to your life?
- What struggles have you overcome?
- How can you incorporate more things you're good at into your everyday life?
- What in life is most important to you, and why?

Exercise: Wheel of Life

We can use the Wheel of Life tool to help us review the core facets of our life and understand which may need more attention so that we feel more fulfilled. This Wheel of Life was adapted from the work of Paul J. Meyer, founder of Success Motivation International.

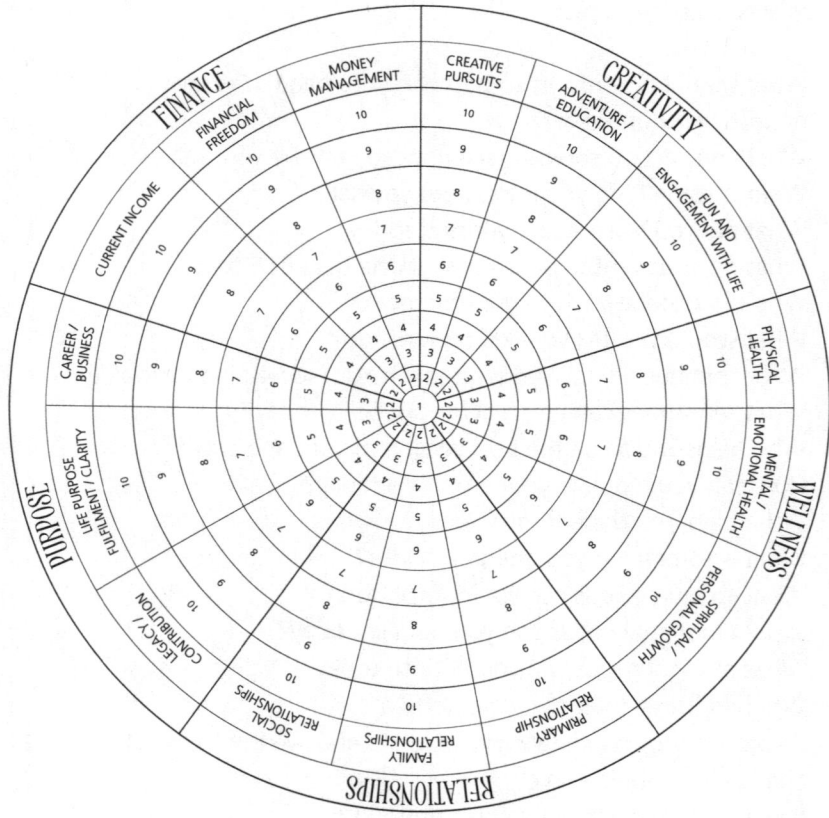

Shade in the segment that represents how you view yourself under each section of the Wheel of Life (1 = 'poor', 10 = 'great'). Once marked, see how your lines link together as a wheel, forming one circle.

The aim is for your circle to be as big and expansive as it possibly can be, representative of a large and abundant life. Through dips and troughs, your markings will uncover which areas you should focus on over the next six to twelve months in order to smooth and widen your circle, make life less of a bumpy ride and help you to feel more fulfilled.

So far in this book, you've learned the basics of therapy and reviewed your motivation to change and set goals. You're well on your way to mastering your mental health, now that you're clearer on what it is you want to achieve.

Before we move ahead, let's check in on your self-esteem. Has it changed since last time?

Chapter 6

Who are you, really?

Self-esteem and living by your values

Self-esteem is the way we view ourselves in the world, and how we think of ourselves as a whole person. People with positive self-esteem take pride in their actions and appearance, believe they are capable of reaching their goals, and believe they are worthy and lovable human beings. Those with low or poor self-esteem think the opposite – that they will not amount to much and that they are not worthy of good things such as love. They may not take pride in their appearance or how they present themselves to the world.

Poor self-esteem can bring about feelings of 'I don't care', which can also negatively influence mental – and even physical – health. Slouching and fatigue are both symptoms that may be expressed when we have poor self-esteem and want to make ourselves seem smaller in the world. While slouching can cause weak muscles and feelings of fatigue, the latter may also be caused by internalising negative emotions, which takes a physiological toll on our bodies – like the upset stomach that might accompany an intense feeling of guilt. Dealing with and processing intense emotions such as the heat of anger and heaviness of sadness can drain us of the energy it takes to live joyfully.

Self-esteem is built from both internal and external factors, and is easily influenced by our perception of how others value us in their lives. This is why it's important to work on our internal self-esteem, so that if something external changes – such as we have a fight with someone we love and they blame us – our self-worth isn't overly compromised. Therapy is a great place to understand ourselves and what we value, and to build a self-identity we can hold in high regard.

What influences self-esteem?

- **Access to basic human rights**: Adding meaning and fulfilment to our lives through socialisation, creativity, growth, goals and connection can help strengthen self-esteem. It's important to note that this is possible only once our basic needs are met, so for people whose physiological, safety and security needs are not being met (as per Maslow's Hierarchy of Needs, page 12), it will be understandably difficult to build positive self-esteem.
- **How we are treated**: Bullying, abuse, trauma, prejudice, stigma, racism, and isolation can all negatively impact self-esteem, especially over prolonged periods or during impressionable times in our lives, such as at high school, when starting a new job, or when a positive outcome does not materialise after we achieve a goal.
- **Societal expectations**: Poor self-esteem impacts people at all stages of life, though teenagers – especially young girls – are even more at risk because of the societal expectations placed upon them from social media, advertising and popular culture to look and act a certain way.
- **The situation we're in**: Self-esteem is very similar to self-confidence. We may feel totally at peace and have high regard for ourselves when we're relaxing with our mates at our favourite hangout location, but feel nervous and small at work when we're doing a presentation, when we are treated poorly, or have just

received a negative response to a task we completed. Increasingly, the way people perceive themselves in comparison to others through social media is also impacting self-esteem, through the pressure to meet unrealistic expectations around wealth, status, body image and aesthetics.

- **Tough moments in life**: Our self-esteem doesn't stay the same throughout our entire lives. Losing our job, having problems at work or school, poor physical health and diagnoses, relationship breakups, even the end of the financial year can all cause a person's self-esteem to wane. As we get knocked down and get up again, our self-esteem will contract and expand, depending on life experiences and interactions with other people.

  Poor mental health can be caused by low self-esteem, especially if we feel down on ourselves for days or weeks at a time. Conversely, having a mental health condition can increase low self-esteem, as we may find it harder to cope with day-to-day activities or take steps to build positive self-esteem.

Self-esteem can present itself positively and negatively, as shown in the table below.

GOOD SELF-ESTEEM	POOR SELF-ESTEEM
Standing tall	Making myself smaller
'I can accomplish anything if I try'	'I'm not good at anything'
'I have friends and family who love me'	'Nobody likes me'
Joining in	Withdrawing from others
Understanding when I am in the right and apologising if I make a mistake	Unfairly blaming myself, even for others' failures
Feeling hopeful	Feeling hopeless
Having good personal hygiene; not letting my appearance be my primary focus	Not caring about my appearance or caring too much about my appearance

GOOD SELF-ESTEEM	POOR SELF-ESTEEM
Responsibly and safely consuming alcohol	Taking drugs or drinking alcohol to 'feel better about myself'
Positive body image: 'I'm attractive', 'I'm strong'	Poor body image: 'I'm ugly', 'I'm weak'
Respecting my own body and others'	Engaging in risky sexual behaviour
Celebrating my accomplishments	Brushing off or belittling my accomplishments
Enjoying social experiences	Avoiding social experiences
Feeling confident and showing it	Being shy, though sometimes acting confident
Being assertive and direct	Having difficulty communicating

A harsh inner critic

Probably the most common way poor self-esteem manifests is through an unkind inner voice. That's when our own internal voice is extremely mean and telling us over and over that we are not good enough, nobody likes us and we'll never amount to anything. Just as a snowball gathers more snow when it rolls down a hill, the negative voice inside becomes louder and louder if we continue to listen. It becomes louder as we feel overwhelmed, judged, distressed or tired, heightening our emotions of anger and sadness.

When we're in a negative headspace, it's easy to believe our inner critic. We will:

- Think everything negative that we say about ourselves is true
- Avoid challenging ourselves
- Focus on our mistakes and shortcomings
- Avoid social and work situations in which we risk being judged by others
- Unconsciously ignore our strengths, abilities and achievements
- Expect the worst
- Feel undeserving of pleasure.

While the above all sounds pretty awful, actually having an inner critic can be good – it helps us to progress, to move forward. Learning to love the process of listening and then asking with curiosity, 'Why am I thinking this?' or 'Why am I talking this way to myself?' can help us to move forward.

Growing your self-worth

Use these tips to expand self-worth and self-efficacy.

- **Set social media boundaries**: Social media platforms are built to keep people engaged. The wish to be voyeurs and see what other people are up to – combined with the addictive nature of Likes and Shares that symbolise an increase in reputation from our peers – draws us in and enables mindless scrolling and comparison. Set timelines to check social media at a time that is better for your mental health, when you're able to deal with whatever feelings it may bring up (often this isn't first thing in the morning). Also consider going through your account and unfollowing anyone whose posts trigger negative emotions when you see them.
- **Speak positively to and about yourself**: Challenge your inner critic and instead speak to yourself as you would speak to a best friend – with love and empathy. While a little awkward at first, an effective way to do this is by standing in front of a mirror and reciting positive affirmations, such as 'I am worthy', 'I am smart', 'I am loved'.
- **Cultivate a creative pursuit**: Finishing projects can improve our self-esteem, especially if the end result is better than our last personal best. Creative outlets such as pottery, drawing or painting are not only meditative but they give you a hit of dopamine because you've accomplished a task.
- **Learn something new**: Accomplishment also comes with learning something new, and by focusing on something outside of ourselves,

we can quieten our inner critic and stop the negative self-talk spiral. What is something you've always had on your list to learn that you could try today?

- **Identify what you're good at**: Knowing what we're good at and having a list of these qualities easily accessible can help remind us of our self-worth and build self-esteem.

- **Celebrate all your milestones**: Recognising and celebrating milestones helps our brains to switch from being hopeless to hopeful, through the practice of gratitude. Celebrate finishing a job early, good weather on the weekend, submitting a project to your teacher on time, the twelve-month anniversary of owning your pet, finishing a good book . . . all these things are wonderful achievements!

- **Separate facts from feelings**: Remember that it's just a bad day, not a bad life. By separating our feelings from the facts, we're able to manage our inner critic and cultivate positive self-esteem. Use the Socratic Questioning (page 115) and RAIN Process (page 177) exercises to practise.

- **Eat and move positively**: Getting our heart rate up releases endorphins and serotonin that improve our mood. Protein contains amino acids, which help our bodies produce the neurotransmitters that carry messages between our nerve cells – including those in our brains – so we can think and learn effectively. Give your brain the best chance to make you feel good by fuelling it well.

- **Find your tribe**: Surrounding ourselves with people who are good to us and treat us well fosters positivity. While it's hard to end friendships and family connections that are not conducive to mental wellbeing, the end result – a happier you – is worth it. Find people in life with similar interests who value what you do. When we're with like-minded people, we're more likely to thrive.

- **Do things you enjoy**: As simple as it sounds, joy comes from the little things. The problem is, it's easy to forget what those little things are and get wrapped up in the day-to-day hamster wheel of living life. Cultivate moments to do things you enjoy by identifying what they are and keeping them close. Use the Five Joyful Things exercise on page 211 as a prompt.

- **Volunteer for others**: Helping other people drowns out our inner critic because the focus is on them and not on us. Volunteering doesn't need to take too much time and can be done locally in our communities – from reading at the library to serving at a soup kitchen. Visit your local council to seek out opportunities.

- **Model yourself after someone you admire**: This isn't a solution to use all the time, but it can help us get on the right track. Identify someone you admire and start to list the reasons why. Are they carefree? Do they appear to not care what others think? Are they always learning, or trying to better themselves? Do you like their style? Do you like how they make you feel? The more laser-focused on their positive qualities and values you can get, the more likely it is that you will get to your own.

- **Accept the ebbs and flows of life**: No one's life is perfect. Everyone experiences the highs of life, and the lows as well – and some will be higher or lower than others. Accepting that life will not be all peaks is a kind of surrender that enables us to understand instinctively that it's okay when things are a little bit terrible. After all, rainbows only come after the rain.

- **Identify what's important to you**: Knowing and living to our values makes it easier to grow internal self-worth – because we know that we're on the right path. Use the values you most identify with in the following pages to remind yourself of your purpose in life, and ignore all the other noise that has no place influencing your self-esteem. When we are content with our true selves and living to our values the best we can, other people's opinions will affect us much less.

What do you value?

Values help us to determine what is most important in our lives and influence our decision making, often giving us purpose in life.

They are the principles by which we live, and we feel our best inside when we stay as true to them as possible. This is particularly true when times get tough, and our values are challenged by peer pressure or circumstances.

Some examples of values in action include:

- A person who values 'creativity' may feel stifled in an office data-entry job.
- A person who values 'connection' may have a big circle of friends they regularly see.
- A person who values 'beauty' may stop to view the sunrise or flowers on their morning walk.
- A person who values 'family' may spend many evenings at home with their family around the dinner table.

Values can mean different things to different people. For example, a person who values 'freedom' may prefer to be single and travel the world. However, for someone else, 'freedom' may represent living without restrictions from their family, government, society or culture.

But remember: values are not always positive. The value of 'victory' may mean winning without care for those around us, and the value of 'loyalty' may cause us to stay in a situation with people who are treating us poorly.

Exercise: Identifying Values

Identifying the values that most resonate with us can help us to home in on what it is we want most in life, and increase our happiness. We're likely to feel more content in our life – and manage adverse situations better – if we can honestly say we're living in line with our values.

Below is a non-exhaustive list of values. Highlight the values below that most resonate with you, and see if you recognise any patterns or commonalities.

Acceptance: Being accepted by other people

Accomplishment: Winning; completing tasks; achieving success

Accountability: Doing what is delegated to you; responsibility

Accuracy: Being correct or precise

Achievement: Doing something successfully with skill, effort, courage

Adaptability: Being able to adjust to new conditions

Altruism: Having selfless concern for others

Ambition: Desire and determination to achieve success

Amusement: Enjoying a sense of humour

Assertiveness: Speaking honestly and respectfully

Attentiveness: Paying close attention

Awareness: Being conscious of what is going on in the world around you

Balance: Distributing activities and time equally

Beauty: Appreciating aesthetics in any form

Boldness: Being willing to take risks and act innovatively

Bravery: Being courageous in character

Brilliance: Having talent or intelligence

Calmness: Being peaceful in mood

Candour: Being open, honest, frank

Capability: Having the power and ability to do certain tasks

Carefulness: Paying attention to avoid mistakes

Certainty: Having conviction, confidence

Challenge: Enjoying tests of ability

Charity: Helping others voluntarily

Cleanliness: Being clean, tidy, hygienic

Cleverness: Being intelligent or quick-witted

Comfort: Having physical ease, cosiness

Commitment: Having dedication to a cause, person, event

Common sense: Exhibiting good judgement

Communication: Sharing and exchanging information

Community: Being with people with shared interests, location, characteristics

Compassion: Having concern for others

Competence: Being able to do something efficiently

Concentration: Being able to focus attention

Confidence: Believing in something; believing in yourself

Connection: Having a relationship with someone or something else

Consciousness: Being aware, responsive

Consistency: Being steady and stable in behaviour

Contentment: Feeling happiness, satisfaction

Contribution: Giving time, effort, items or money to others

Control: Having power, behavioural influence

Conviction: Having firmly held beliefs, opinions

Cooperation: Working with others towards one goal

Courage: Having strength when faced with fear, pain, grief

Courtesy: Being polite with others

Creation: Bringing something into existence

Creativity: Having inventiveness, imagination

Credibility: Being trusted, believed

Curiosity: Wanting to learn, know

Decisiveness: Being a quick and confident decision maker

Dedication: Being committed to a task or purpose

Dependability: Being trustworthy and reliable

Determination: Having a firmness of purpose

Devotion: Feeling love or loyalty for a person or activity; religious worship

Dignity: Being worthy of honour or respect

Discipline: Obeying rules, codes of behaviour

Discovery: Finding and learning something new

Drive: Having ambition, hunger to move forward

Effectiveness: Achieving success

Efficiency: Being well organised, competent

Empathy: Understanding and sharing feelings with others

Empowerment: Increasing and giving power, control

Endurance: Withstanding difficult situations, processes

Energy: Having strength and vitality

Enjoyment: Taking pleasure in a task

Enthusiasm: Feeling eager enjoyment, interest

Equality: Believing in equal status, rights, opportunities

Ethicalness: Having a strong sense of fairness and morality

Excellence: Being extremely good or outstanding in a given area

Experience: Practically engaging with events and facts

Exploration: Examining unfamiliar areas, ideas

Expression: Making thoughts and feelings known

Fairness: Believing in impartiality and just treatment for all

Faith: Having complete trust and confidence; belief in religion

Fame: Being known by many

Family: Connecting with genetic or chosen close relatives

Fearlessness: Being free from anxiety or fear

Ferociousness: Possessing extreme power or force in activity

Fidelity: Being faithful to a person or cause

Focus: Having determination, an inability to be distracted

Foresight: Being able to predict what may be needed in future

Fortitude: Having strength, especially in adversity

Freedom: Being unrestricted by people, places, things

Friendship: Having a meaningful connection with friends

Fun: Experiencing enjoyment, amusement, lighthearted pleasures

Generosity: Giving to others by sharing gifts, skills or time

Goodness: Being morally good, virtuous

Grace: Showing courteous goodwill; having elegance of movement

Gratitude: Being thankful, appreciative

Greatness: Having distinction, eminence

Growth: Improving or changing positively over time

Happiness: Feeling contentment, joy

Hard work: Paying your dues; putting in effort; endurance

Harmony: Forming a pleasing, consistent whole; balance

Health: Experiencing physical, emotional wellbeing

Honesty: Being truthful

Honour: Knowing and doing what is morally right

Hope: Desiring and believing in a particular thing in the future

Humility: Having a modest opinion of yourself

Imagination: Using your mind to be creative, resourceful

Improvement: Making yourself and your situations better

Independence: Not relying on others; being free

Individuality: Distinguishing yourself from others through quality or character

Innovation: Having new ideas, processes, methods

Insightfulness: Having accurate and deep understanding; being perceptive

Inspiration: Giving positive, creative feelings

Integrity: Being honest; having moral principles

Intelligence: Acquiring and applying skills and knowledge

Intensity: Having strength and power

Intuition: Being instinctual

Irreverence: Not taking things too seriously

Joy: Experiencing happiness, great pleasure

Justice: Believing in fairness and equality for all

Kindness: Being friendly, generous, considerate

Knowledge: Acquiring facts, information, skills

Lawfulness: Following the rules set by society, especially law enforcement

Leadership: Guiding within a group or organisation; hierarchy

Learning: Acquiring knowledge through study, experience or being taught

Logic: Believing in reasoning, fact

Love: Feeling intense affection for friends, family, pets, things

Loyalty: Having strong feelings of support, allegiance

Mastery: Having comprehensive knowledge in a particular subject; having control over something

Maturity: Acting your age, or wise beyond your years

Meaning: Finding an important or worthwhile quality; having purpose

Moderation: Avoiding extremes

Motivation: Having reasons to act or behave in certain ways

Openness: Withholding no secrets; being frank

Optimism: Having hopefulness and confidence about the future

Order: Preferring arrangements of sequences, patterns, methods

Organisation: Planning, arranging

Originality: Being novel, unusual; thinking independently, creatively

Passion: Feeling strong emotion, usually positive

Patience: Tolerating delays, problems and suffering without becoming annoyed

Peace: Being free from disturbance; calmness

Performance: Presenting skills or talents; entertaining a crowd

Persistence: Continuing in spite of difficulty

Playfulness: Being lighthearted; having fun

Poise: Having gracefulness, elegance

Potential: Having latent qualities or abilities that develop, leading to future success

Power: Influencing people or events

Presentness: Living in the here and now

Productivity: Doing actions to create outputs

Professionalism: Acting appropriately in the workplace

Prosperity: Having success; thriving

Purpose: Feeling a sense of resolve or determination; knowing why you are doing something

Quality: Appreciating premium or well-crafted things

Realism: Accepting situations; representing people or things accurately

Reason: Thinking, understanding and forming judgements logically

Recognition: Receiving appreciation or acclaim for an achievement, service, ability

Recreation: Prioritising leisure activities

Respect: Receiving admiration elicited by abilities, qualities, achievements

Responsibility: Taking ownership of actions or duties

Restraint: Moderating behaviour; exercising self-control

Results: Achieving tangible outcomes following activity

Reverence: Holding regard for others, being respectful

Rigour: Being extremely thorough, careful

Risk: Exposing yourself to danger; taking chances

Satisfaction: Fulfillment of wishes, expectations, needs

Security: Being free from danger or threat

Self-reliance: Not relying on another person

Selflessness: Caring more for others' needs and wants than your own

Sensitivity: Being caring, responsive

Serenity: Being calm, peaceful, untroubled

Service: Helping others; doing work for others

Sharing: Using or enjoying something with others

Silence: Experiencing an absence of sound, distractions

Simplicity: Appreciating minimalism and clarity

Sincerity: Being genuine; without pretence or deceit

Skill: Doing something well and often

Solitude: Having alone time

Spirituality: Being concerned with the human spirit as opposed to physical things

Spontaneity: Acting without planning

Stability: Being steady and dependable

Status: Having a high social or professional position

Stewardship: Guiding or taking care of a group, organisation or cause

Strength: Having great fortitude under pressure

Structure: Prioritising organisation and planning

Success: Accomplishing an aim; fulfilling a purpose

Support: Giving assistance, especially financial or emotional

Surprise: Experiencing unexpected or astonishing events

Sustainability: Avoiding the depletion of natural resources

Talent: Having natural aptitude or skill

Teamwork: Effectively and efficiently working in a group

Thoroughness: Acting with great care and attention to detail

Thoughtfulness: Being considerate of the needs of others

Timeliness: Being prompt, on time

Tolerance: Being accepting of the beliefs, behaviours and actions of others

Toughness: Being able to cope in difficult situations

Tradition: Upholding beliefs and customs from previous generations

Tranquillity: Having a sense of calm

Transparency: Being open, frank

Trustworthiness: Being reliable, earning the confidence of others

Truth: Being honest; preferring facts, reality

Understanding: Having sympathetic awareness

Uniqueness: Being one of a kind

Unity: Being part of a complex whole

Valour: Having courage in the face of danger

Victory: Experiencing success, triumph, winning

Vigour: Having physical strength, good health

Vision: Planning with imagination or wisdom

Vitality: Being strong and active; having energy

Wealth: Earning or having abundant money or possessions

———

Some of these values overlap, with meanings going hand in hand. Did you notice any recurring themes in the values you chose to highlight?

Now fill in the table below to identify which of the values above matter most to you.

Which core personal values do you CURRENTLY live by the most?

1. _____ because _____

2. _____ because _____

3. _____ because _____

Which core personal values do you most WISH you lived by?

1. _____ because _____

2. _____ because _____

3. _____ because _____

Which core personal values do you LEAST identify with?

1. _____ because _____

1. _____ because _____

1. _____ because _____

Who or what INFORMS each of your core values?
(e.g. family, friends, faith, a mentor, a TV character, your culture . . .)

1. _____ because _____

1. _____ because _____

1. _____ because _____

When we live true to our values, we feel more content and relaxed. When we live against our values, we can feel unbalanced, unhappy and discontented. Do the values you currently live by match the ones you wished you live by? What changes could you put in place to live your life closer to the values you hold most highly?

When we know why we are who we are, we can often separate ourselves from negative actions and ways of thinking simply by saying to ourselves, 'This does not align with my values.' In fact, values can act as a kind of 'North Star', helping us to create the kind of life we dream of – when we live by them.

When we live in line with our values, we are able to deal with adverse moments in life much more easily. This doesn't mean we will never feel sadness or moments of disappointment, but it does mean that when those moments come, they won't utterly overwhelm us. Instead, we'll be able to accept them, hold space for them and question whether they align with our values. If they don't, then we can move past them more easily.

Identifying positive qualities

Now that you've identified the values that matter most to you, let's use this momentum to build your self-worth and identify your positive qualities. For some of us, this is really hard to do off the cuff – we may feel awkward writing our Instagram bios, let alone talking about all the positive things we can offer. It can be hard to identify positive qualities in ourselves unless we truly go looking for them.

Exercise: My Positive Qualities

Use the table below to uncover your most positive qualities, and keep it close for those days your inner critic is at its loudest.

MY POSITIVE QUALITIES	
Reasons I like myself . . .	
My positive qualities . . .	

In my life, I have achieved . . .	
Talents I have . . .	
Skills I've acquired in my life . . .	
Traits other people like and value about me . . .	
Positive traits in other people that I share . . .	
The positives I have but often forget about or ignore . . .	
Some bad things that I am not . . .	
Someone who cares about me would describe me as . . .	

Many people find it incredibly hard to speak positively about themselves. We're often conditioned not to be overtly proud or 'show off' when we are at school, and this has impacts when we enter the workforce and need to write our own LinkedIn biographies or list our positive traits at job interviews. If you found the above exercise a little difficult, you can work on accepting your good qualities through repetition. Remind yourself that it's okay to know your positive traits and be proud of them, to love those aspects of yourself, and to recognise when you do something really well. By doing so, you'll build your self-esteem – and that's definitely worth showing off!

Time for another self-esteem check in. How are you feeling?

Chapter 7

Hello, little one

Connecting with your inner child

Who are you when you are your truest self and living to those values? Without pretence, or airs and graces? Without the cool labels and the status-symbol bag or car? Who are you deep within, when stripped back and bare?

The average adult makes a huge 35,000 decisions every day.[1] Too often we can go through life without thinking about why we're making these decisions, as if we are operating on muscle memory alone. But whose muscle memory is it?

Our inner child is the part of us that has been picking up messages long before we could fully process what was going on, emotionally and mentally. They are a part of our subconscious, which holds our memories, our emotions, our beliefs about the past, and our hopes and dreams for the future. The inner child helped form us into the type of person we are today, but it can also be a wounded part of us, and may cause us to emotionally (over)react to certain scenarios that others don't find as triggering. They're someone we need to meet.

Who is the inner child?

When we're young, and we're learning from the world and people around us, our emotional coping abilities are limited. If we are threatened or experience a trauma of some sort at this young age, we cannot properly process what is happening. When we are adults, we may seem to have 'gotten over' that trauma, but there's still a part of us that reacts like a child when threatened or upset by interpersonal relationships. That childlike part of us is known as our inner child. According to counsellor and author John Bradshaw, 'the wounded inner child of the past is the major source of [today's] human misery.'[2]

The wounds Bradshaw is talking about are the unmet emotional, physical and spiritual needs from our childhood that continue to threaten our present selves through our subconscious. For example, if we have been shamed for being too emotional as a young child, we may make an effort to always be happy and cheerful in a group scenario and never show vulnerability. In other words, we hide that need – to feel our emotions – that we suppressed as a child and instead try to be strong for other people, neglecting our inner child. If, as a child, we only received love from our parents when we achieved goals, we may become the kind of adult who views achieving as the only way to earn love, and who seeks external validation to build feelings of self-worth, leaning into perfectionist tendencies.

It is hard to feel like our whole, truest self when the needs of our inner child are still not being met, even in adulthood.

Think of the cutest little two-year-old character you've ever seen on television (or in real life!). They're looking up at you from close to the ground, a smaller version of you. Your eyes are mirrors to theirs, your hair a grown-up style of their own. They pull on your shirt hem and ask:

- Why is the sky blue?
- Why does the truck drive?
- Why do we have to go to work?
- Why should I use my manners?

When thrown at us all at once, many 'whys' can be overwhelming and even annoying. But what if we made a game with our inner child and, instead of asking questions in lots of different directions, stayed on one line of questioning? What if we dug deeper and deeper into one particular 'why':

- Why am I the way that I am?

Our inner child remembers all the good and bad experiences we have had since we were little, often leaving hints for us of what these may be, such as when we experience feelings that we can't quite place.[3] For instance, we may get a feeling of joy when we smell gardenias but not know why, when in fact our inner child (our subconscious self) remembers that our grandmother's perfume smelled like gardenias when she handed us our favourite teddy bear as a third-birthday present. Or we may get scared and have trouble breathing when we hear a group of motorcycles roaring up the freeway and not understand where that fear comes from. Our inner child, though, remembers the multiple-motorcycle accident our family saw on the way to our holiday cabin one summer when we were young. Or we may feel shame around failing a group activity at university and not quite know why this failure is impacting us so much more than it seems to be impacting the other group members. Our inner child remembers that we were berated and denied love whenever we brought home anything less than a 'B' grade.

The reason this subconscious self is called the 'inner child' is because it is always within us. If we're feeling stuck or disheartened with work, parenting, relationships, finances or any other area of our lives, there's a likelihood our inner child needs some attention – someone to make them feel safe.

Qualities of the inner child

Our inner child has core needs and qualities that must be nurtured so that we can live as our authentic selves in the present day. When these needs are met, we will feel as though we're living congruently, inside and out.

CORE NEEDS OF OUR INNER CHILD	QUALITIES OF OUR NURTURED INNER CHILD
Connection: Positive relationships with family, friends	'I feel safe'
	'I am open to many different perspectives'
Significance: Understanding of sense of self and position in the world	'I am creative'
	'I practise self-care'
Safety: Ability to express without judgement	'I believe there is possibility in all moments'
Freedom: Autonomy to choose what's best for self	'I use my imagination'
	'I honour the boundaries of others'
Stimulation: Desire to learn	'I observe without judgement'
Growth: Ability to face challenges and learn from them	'I validate myself'
Variety: Openness to new experiences	'I am enough'
	'I enjoy play'
Love: Security to be vulnerable with others	'I honour my own boundaries'

Exercise: Inner Child

The following exercise will help you to identify the unmet needs of your inner child and focus in on how you can nurture them. Use the template on page 98 and pretend it is a young version of yourself (or, better yet, stick a photo of yourself as a young child on top of the graphic below).

- What is their name? Perhaps it's a nickname you had as a kid. Write this above their head in big letters.
- How do they feel? Draw a face on your inner child that captures their emotions.

- What brings your inner child joy? Draw a balloon to their left side and inside it write down three things that make them happy.
- What makes them sad? Draw a storm cloud to their right side and fill it with three things that hurt them.
- What does your inner child hope, dream and wish for? Write it anywhere on the page and draw a big star around it.
- What does your inner child worry about? Write their worries underneath their feet.
- How does your inner child receive love? Draw a heart on their chest, and inside it write down what makes them feel most loved.
- What makes them unique? Draw some physical features, clothing, objects or accessories that represent your inner child's unique qualities and interests.
- Finally, choose a space anywhere on the page and write in big capital letters: 'I AM ENOUGH'.

Now make a copy of your inner child template and put it somewhere visible in your bedroom or office. What would you like to say to them? What do you wish they knew? What things can you do today that would make your inner child happy? If you are feeling stuck, you might be able to look at them and help them conquer the sadness and worry beneath their feet, assisting them to reach the joy and dreams surrounding them, using the tips and tricks you've learned throughout *Paperback Therapy* so far.

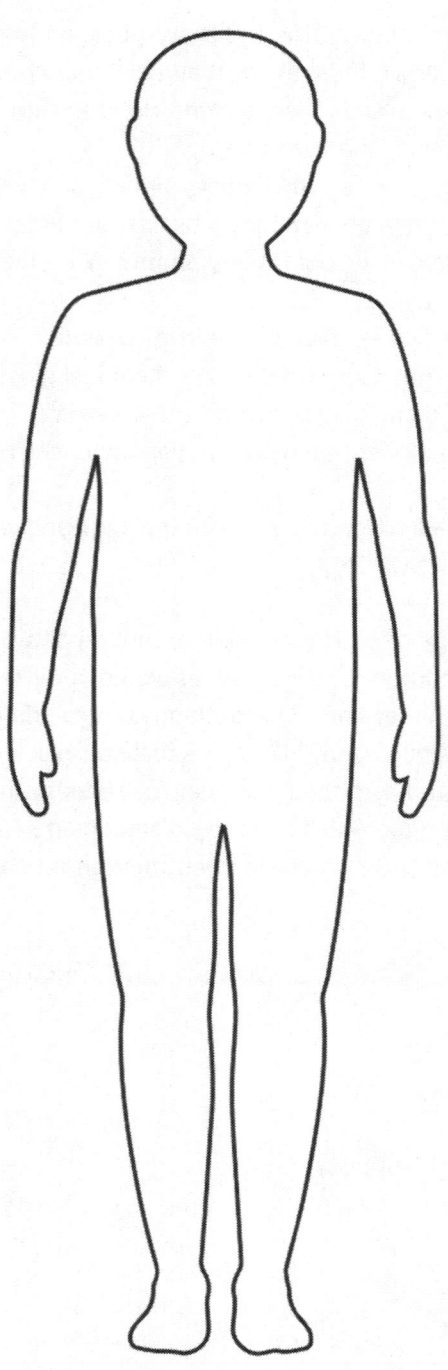

Ways to nurture our inner child

Now our inner child has been acknowledged, it's time to nurture them and provide them with the love and care they deserve. We can nurture our inner child by:

- Making space and enabling the freedom to do whatever feels best
- Taking time to play
- Having rest when it's needed
- Being seen and heard
- Honouring our own boundaries
- Observing our emotions without judgement
- Practising disciplined self-care
- Creating, e.g. by writing, drawing, painting, sculpting.

I nurture my inner child through self-validation, self-compassion, self-acceptance and self-soothing! Getting proper help and support that respects me, validates me, but also is honest and encouraging of positive and effective behaviours. Showing myself respect and nurture by caring for myself like I would for a best friend or me as a child – with kindness, openness, encouragement, compassion and love.

**Ashira, 26
Melbourne, Victoria**

Okay, but why?

Here's an example of how we may use the 'Why?' question technique to unstick a feeling our inner child is presenting to us.

- Daisy gets more nervous than others when asked to do a presentation for work. *Why?*
- Because Daisy is afraid her colleagues will think she's dumb. *Why?*

- Because Daisy's supposed 'friends' used to call her dumb as a kid. *Why?*
- Because Daisy received the lowest grades at school. *Why?*
- Because Daisy didn't have time to study like her friends. *Why?*
- Because Daisy had to work extra hours to support her family. *Why?*
- Because Daisy's parents were both sick when she was growing up, so she raised her siblings. *Why?*
- Because family is more important than anything to Daisy.

We can tell from Daisy's experience that she values family because as a child she put them first. We can also see that she fears being 'seen' academically or through work, and that this is because her friends – the people who she hoped would support her – called her names linked to her academic results. Thus, Daisy's inner child feels like an under-achiever and forces present-world Daisy to shy away from the spotlight when it comes to work.

After Daisy drills down and discovers that her nervousness about presentations stems from an experience many years prior, and realises that her family is more important than anything, she can switch her thinking to help rather than hinder her presentations. Instead of thinking, 'I can't do this presentation because I will look dumb in front of my colleagues,' Daisy can switch her thinking to, 'I am enough, and I am doing this presentation so I can continue to provide for my family.'

Daisy's values helped her to discover what really matters by asking the question 'Why?' When we look inside to the innermost drivers of our actions and reactions (our emotions), our inner child is often in the front seat. When we listen to them and give them what they want, they can help us to be healthier and happier, and uncover the answer to the question 'Why do I feel the way that I feel?'

———

The concept of the Inner Child can be a tricky one to understand, but it can be a great way to learn self-compassion once we do. Giving ourselves the love and attention our littlest selves deserve can make it easier for us to forgive our previous behaviours and move forward with a more direct, important purpose – our 'why'.

Chapter 8

All the feels

The mind–body connection and mastering your emotions

Have you ever felt hot and antsy after picking a fight with your mum? Maybe you've experienced butterflies in your tummy before a speech, or a heaviness in your body after losing someone you love? These are all demonstrations of how emotions and physical feelings can go hand in hand, and being able to recognise these is an important step in managing our mental wellbeing.

Think, feel, behave

Our body is so linked to our emotions that some of us can identify how we feel from the physical manifestation of our emotion before we can actually name our feelings. Physical symptoms – such as tight chests, clenched jaws or flushed faces – are all signs of feeling an intense emotion.

Importantly, not all physical symptoms of emotions are negative. The overwhelming warmth and lightness of happiness and love, for instance, play off the occasional heavy, weighted feeling that sits in our tummy when feeling dread. Therapists can help us become better attuned to ourselves by making sense of all our physical emotional symptoms, showing us tricks to help us push the unhelpful ones away and recognise with gratitude those that make us feel good.

The first step to understanding our mind–body connection is to engage in respectful curiosity. This is where we non-judgementally ask ourselves what it is we're feeling; where it is in our body; what colour it may be; and what its shape, size or texture is. For instance, we may feel sadness deep in our tummy. It may feel dark-grey, fluid and weighted, like a heavy cloud that's ready to break, and it may slowly swirl, making us uncomfortable.

While our emotions may make us feel a little uncomfortable, it's important not to criticise ourselves when we feel them. Everyone feels emotions and most people feel them in a very similar way. When we criticise ourselves and believe that we shouldn't feel a certain way, this amplifies our emotional pain, adding shame, embarrassment and pity on top of the core emotion we are feeling. Not fun at all.

To combat the pile-on of negative emotion, we can treat ourselves as we would a friend we care for. We wouldn't ever tell a mate who was feeling down that they had no right to feel that way – and so we shouldn't tell ourselves that either. Instead, we can build our self-esteem by acknowledging our emotions with a positive attitude, saying, 'I am feeling sad. It's okay that I feel this way, I'm allowed to.'

And then we sit with that emotion.

That means not trying to immediately make ourselves feel better or push away our feelings. While blocking these emotions or distracting ourselves from them by doing other (sometimes risky) activities may seem enticing, this only provides temporary relief.

While emotions may be felt on the inside, they can also manifest as physical symptoms that those around us can see. When we're embarrassed, we may flush red in the face; our eyes may well up with tears when we're sad; we may become fidgety when we're anxious; and we might inadvertently look down to avoid eye contact when ashamed. These physical symptoms are harder to hide, and thus can impact our self-esteem when they are noticed, such as during an interview or presentation, or just before the first kiss with someone we've liked for a while.

Acknowledging our emotions doesn't mean sitting and wallowing in them. If we're sad, it's certainly tempting to retreat from our friends and spend more time alone doing things that distract us from our emotions, such as watching television and mindlessly scrolling through Instagram. But this isn't helpful. In fact, it can make us feel even sadder because we feel disengaged from enjoyment and our social support – friends and family.

> To get rid of our feelings is like trying to push a beach ball underwater – with a bit of effort we might push it under the surface for a moment, but it will keep popping back up. To go back to the idea of treating ourselves like a friend, if a friend told us they were anxious we wouldn't ignore that comment and immediately try to distract them – we might allow some space in the conversation to talk about why they are feeling this way, how long it has been going on for, and how it is impacting them. It can be helpful to allow some space to experience and process our own emotions in this way too.
>
> **Melissa Burgess, clinical psychologist**

There are ways we can learn to control our emotions a bit better, and to *respond* instead of *react* to them. Learning to be calmer in a crisis or hold back tears until we're in a more comfortable setting can help diffuse our emotions and stop them from getting the better of us.

The trick here is to do the opposite of what you want to do (e.g. stay inside and wallow) by doing something that is active and/or social (e.g. going for a walk with a mate).

———

Exercise: Opposite Actions

Popular in dialectical behaviour therapy, the Opposite Actions task forces an end to a negative pattern by encouraging you to do the opposite of what is usual. As your response to an emotion is biologically wired, it takes conscious thought to change your habits and choose to take the opposite action.

Here are some examples of negative feelings, and the common actions (behaviours) associated with them.

EMOTION	COMMON ACTIONS
Anxiety	Fill our calendar, stay busy
Anger	Scream, punch, kick
Fear	Hide, run, avoid the fear-inducing thing or activity, look away
Guilt	Avoid other people, eat unhealthy foods
Sadness	Retreat from others, stay in bed, eat unhealthy food or stop eating altogether
Shame	Put head down, isolate from others, try to hide

The above feelings and actions are all valid. However, if you want a different, more resilient outcome, you can choose to do the opposite action and reap the reward of a positive feeling.

NEGATIVE FEELING	COMMON ACTIONS	OPPOSITE ACTION	POSITIVE FEELING
Anxiety	Fill our calendar, stay busy	Leave Sundays free for 'me' time or to catch up on life admin	Calmness

NEGATIVE FEELING	COMMON ACTIONS	OPPOSITE ACTION	POSITIVE FEELING
Anger	Scream, punch, kick	Deep breathe with eyes closed, walk away	Peacefulness
Fear	Hide, run, avoid the fear-inducing thing or activity, look away	Stand up tall, engage with the fear-inducing thing or activity	Confidence
Guilt	Avoid other people, eat unhealthy foods	Own up to actions, acknowledge mistakes made	Satisfaction
Sadness	Retreat from others, stay in bed, eat unhealthy food or stop eating altogether	Visit friends or family, go for a walk, eat a nourishing meal	Happiness
Shame	Put head down, isolate from others, try to hide	Stand up tall, surround yourself with others	Pride

The more you do the opposite actions, the more your brain wires itself to respond in this way. Below is a list of additional negative feelings you may experience, along with their common actions. Build resilience by adding the opposite action you could take next time to switch your feelings from negative to positive. Add to the blank boxes at the bottom of the table when you feel a feeling that's not listed.

NEGATIVE FEELING	COMMON ACTIONS	OPPOSITE ACTION	POSITIVE FEELING
Boredom	Scroll mindlessly on social media, eat or snack when not hungry		Excitement
Envy	Compare, criticise		Gratitude
Frustration	Give up, avoid the task		Competence
Nervousness	Hide away, avoid the action, cancel the event		Calmness
Worthlessness	Avoid others, behave destructively, self-harm		Worthiness

The common emotions above can be easy to manage physically. Trauma, however, is psychologically and physiologically stored and can be much more difficult to manage. Manifesting as a fight-or-flight reflex response when activated, a trauma response often looks like itching to get away, anxious fidgeting, a pounding heart or sweating. The freeze response is also common if we experience trauma, manifesting as the inability to get out of bed, the inability to move, or freezing when triggered by an activity that reminds us of our traumatic experience (e.g. if we hear car tyres squeal after experiencing our own car accident). This impacts our executive functioning, which helps us to be present and interact meaningfully with the world.

Traumatic emotions – often signs of post-traumatic stress – can stay in the body, but we don't always make the connection between our feelings and the past trauma that may be responsible. Constant headaches, chronic pain, jumpiness and dissociation (the feeling that we are disconnected from ourselves and the world around us) are all examples of how trauma can be held in the body, even when we feel as though we are 'over' the traumatic experience itself. Although these effects are often triggered when we're reminded of a traumatic event, at times they can seem to come out of the blue, and this can cause us to attribute our memory issues, tight chest, trouble sleeping, brain fog or muscle tension to everyday stress and tiredness. In fact, experiencing trauma can shrink our 'window of tolerance' – the ability to handle stressful situations without them becoming overwhelming.

Trauma-informed therapists assist clients to manage emotions in the body through evidence-based methods like prolonged exposure therapy or cognitive behaviour therapy, helping us to separate ourselves from the trauma-inducing activity. Given the way trauma can live dormant inside our body, body work is especially popular in assisting in healing, as it helps us recognise emotions we may not logically or readily understand to be impacting us. Body work techniques include trauma-informed yoga, where the practitioner is trained in trauma responses and the yoga studio is safe for participants to address feelings of disconnection from their body in a guided practice, and somatic therapy, which specifically focuses on how our body holds and expresses experiences. Through such practices, and talk therapy, the symptoms of trauma in our body can be processed, our nervous system regulated, and we can draw closer to an end goal of positively re-engaging with the world.

A simple way to externalise an emotion is to use curiosity to describe it (even putting a name to it!), to take back control. In doing this, you can more easily consider the emotion an invasion rather than an intrinsic part of you, making it something you can more easily disconnect from yourself.

Exercise: Externalising Emotions

Here is an example of how you could externalise your emotions. The more questions you ask, the more detail you will share, separating yourself from the negative feeling. Column one is a prompt for you, while column two shows examples of someone feeling sad.

Draw your emotion in the first box as you work through the prompts.

THE EMOTION I FEEL INSIDE	EXAMPLE: 'SADNESS'
• Where are you feeling the emotion?	• *I feel it over my chest.*
• Let's take it out of your body and put it in the room – where is it?	• *It's over there, hovering above the floor.*

THE EMOTION I FEEL INSIDE	EXAMPLE: 'SADNESS'
• What colour is the emotion? Is it all one colour or does it have many?	• *It's grey, lots of different shades, like a puddle or cloud – but heavy.*
• What does it feel like? Is it heavy or light? Is it fuzzy or smooth?	• *It's heavy and smooth, almost wet.*
• Can you see through your emotion? Is it opaque or transparent?	• *I can see through some parts and not others, more like a cloud.*
• Does it look dry or wet?	• *It's wet, like it's full of tears.*
• Is it still or is it moving? How is it moving?	• *No, it's moving a little. Slowly and rhythmically, like blubber but not bouncing, just going all over the place. Fluid!*
• Does it have a name?	• *I'll call it Mr Sad.*
• What is [name] telling you to do? What does it want from you?	• *Mr Sad wants me to stay inside and under the covers, to not see my friends and to withdraw from everything. He wants me to always be there, because he's always there.*
• What do you want to say to [name]?	• *Mr Sad, I see you and I'm sorry you're here, but I am going to go out and see my friends anyway, because I am not a sad person – I am just a bit sad when we're together. You stay here, I'm going out.*

Once the emotion is externalised, you can ask questions that continue to position the emotion outside of you and uncover ways it has previously held you back, or ways in which you have successfully managed your emotion in the past. By reminding ourselves that we have moved away from the feeling before, we will realise that we can do so again. For example, in relation to Mr Sad (above), you might consider:

- How has Mr Sad restricted your life previously?
- When you have control of Mr Sad, how does he hook you back in?
- How is Mr Sad holding you back?
- What is helping Mr Sad to continue making problems for you?
- What do you think Mr Sad would do as a last-ditch effort to stay in your life, as you become stronger against him?
- How have you defeated Mr Sad in the past?
- Who in your life does Mr Sad really not like?

The above questions enable you to uncover who your social supports are, what 'feeds' the negative emotion (e.g. staying in bed all day), and what continues to separate Mr Sad from you as an individual. You are not sad; you are a person who is troubled by being sad (i.e. Mr Sad), and sometimes sadness (i.e. Mr Sad) gets control of you at times.

The gut–brain axis

Ever heard the saying 'Trust your gut'? It may be a cliche, but it's actually grounded in science – the link between our mind and our gut is strong, thanks to one special nerve: the vagus nerve.

The vagus nerve connects our gastrointestinal tract to our central nervous system through spinal pathways, sending messages in both directions. However, the conversation is not equally weighted. Research shows only 20 per cent of nerve signals get from our brain to our gut, versus 80 per cent of nerve signals travelling from gut to brain.[1] The health of our gut microbiome – that is, the good bacteria and other microorganisms that live in our intestines and help us to digest fibre, regulate our immune system and control our brain health – can therefore seriously impact our mental and emotional wellbeing.

Symptoms of irritable bowel syndrome, taking strong antibiotics, consuming too many artificially sweetened foods, stress, lack of quality sleep, drinking or smoking too much, and not eating a diverse range of foods can all impact our gut health – and thus our minds. Speak with your doctor about your gut health to see if a probiotic might support your gastrointestinal, emotional and mental wellbeing. It could help strengthen your gut instinct!

Knowing that the body and the mind are so closely linked can help us to respond to bodily feelings in a way that is emotionally mindful. Next time you feel a little niggle in your tummy or catch yourself slumping down in a chair, take a beat and check inwards to ask yourself what may be causing these feelings. Is something off in your world? Do you feel threatened? Are you embarrassed about something? By checking in and putting a cause to our feelings, we can often become better attuned to our emotions – and thus learn how to master them.

Chapter 9

Meaningful connections

Managing interpersonal relationships

'Birds of a feather flock together', 'You are the average of the five people you spend the most time with', 'You can tell a lot about a person by the company they keep' . . . there are so many well-known phrases about the importance of the people we are closest to, and how those relationships can shape our lives. And there's a reason for that. While the nature-versus-nurture debate – about whether genetics or our environmental factors and experiences have more of an impact on our characteristics – is a hot one, there's no denying that the people we spend time with shape our belief systems, our values and our happiness.

The people we connect with, whether casually or more meaning-fully, make up our interpersonal relationships. We have relationships with everyone from our partners, friends, family and colleagues, through to our kid's teacher, the local barista and the veterinarian. Our interactions with all these individuals are meaningful to our lives, because they keep us plugged into our community, something – as you'll know by this point in *Paperback Therapy* – that is important to our emotional, social and physical health. The opposite of *inter*personal relationships is *intra*personal relationships, the one we have with ourselves.

Interpersonal relationships help give us purpose and combat loneliness. Without them, our emotional health will be impacted, leaving us feeling lost. Think about how good you feel when your barista remembers your order or says hello to you by name, or when your bus driver wishes you a happy weekend as you tap off on a Friday afternoon. All these tiny interactions make us feel seen in the world.

For the purposes of this chapter, we'll focus on deeper relationships – friendships, romantic relationships, and relationships with our families. But never discount the impact a smile to a stranger on your morning walk can have.

Friends forever . . . ?

From a very early age, we are led to cultivate friendships. As babies, we hang out with the kids of our parents' friends. In school, we have buddy systems and play dates and sleepovers. When we're adults, we have uni friends, work friends, friends we met on our gap year. Some of these friendships last a lifetime; others are strong only during particular seasons of our lives, and then we lose touch.

Many friendships follow the stage theory, coined by psychologist George Levinger, comprising five stages: acquaintance, build-up, continuation, deterioration and ending (termination). The aim is to maintain the 'continuation' phase for most of our relationships – that's where lifelong friendships are formed. Sometimes, though, relationships aren't healthy, and we need to move to the termination phase in order to protect our self-worth.[1]

Comparison and jealousy are common issues to arise in friendships, especially as we move through different life stages. Both stem from feelings of competitiveness, and can be related to physical appearance, financial success, life milestones (houses, babies, weddings, partners) and more. Meaningful friendship comes from being happy for our mates when they achieve success, but that's not always our first emotion. The trick is to not allow jealousy to fester and grow – acknowledge the feeling internally ('I am feeling very bitter about her promotion'), be curious about where it's coming from ('It must be because I have been trying for a promotion of my own'), then untie it from your friendship ('I can be happy for her, while also still trying for a promotion'). Simran Kaur, co-founder of Girls That Invest, once summed it up on Instagram: 'Seeing other people's success is confirmation of my own possibilities.'[2]

Another regular source of discontent in friendships is inconsistency, especially around the level of attention the relationship receives. For instance, if we feel we're always the first one to facilitate catch-ups, it can breed resentment and make us wonder if the other person wants to be our friend as much as we want to be theirs. When these kinds of thoughts arise in a friendship – or any relationship – it can be useful to take a step back and analyse our thoughts and feelings. Try the Socratic Questioning exercise below to investigate your thoughts and feelings about a relationship that is important to you.

Exercise: Socratic Questioning

When an unwanted thought pops into your mind repetitively, it can be distressing. Intrusive thoughts can be rational ('I miss my ex-girlfriend') or irrational ('I could easily steal this skirt'), but one thing they have in common is that people often don't want them to continue cropping up.

Used often in cognitive behaviour therapy, Socratic Questioning challenges irrational thoughts so that we realise just how unhelpful these thoughts can be, and can put a stop to them. The name 'Socratic Questioning' comes from the Greek philosopher Socrates, who believed thoughtful questioning enables us to logically review ideas and determine their validity.

Here is an example of Socratic Questioning being used on the irrational thought of 'My best friend doesn't want to be friends with me anymore.'

My intrusive thought is . . .	Indi doesn't like me anymore and doesn't want to be friends.
What evidence is there for this thought?	I've texted them three times and not heard back.
	I saw them on social media with Alissar.
What evidence is there against this thought?	They sent me a birthday card last week.
	They are sending me memes on Instagram.
Am I really looking at all the evidence, or only that which supports my thought?	Indi told me last week that they were busy at work, so maybe that's why they've not contacted me via text.
	Indi's parents are in town too, and so they're playing tour guide.
	Alissar knows Indi's parents – she used to live next door to them when they were kids.
Am I misinterpreting the evidence?	Perhaps, yes. There is more evidence against my thought.
Is this thought based on facts? Or is it based on feelings?	No, feelings. I miss Indi and am focusing on them not responding to me this week.
What might other people who know the evidence think? Is it different from my thought?	Yes, they would say Indi is just busy at the moment and that they will get back to me soon.
Is this a habitual thought I've had before? Why?	Occasionally. I was bullied in high school and I was exiled from my friendship group.
	I fear this may happen again with Indi.
Is this my own thought or did I get it from someone else? If the latter, are they reliable?	It is my own thought, informed by my high school experience.
Is this thought a *likely* scenario or is it the *worst-case* scenario?	This is the worst-case scenario, and – looking at the evidence – is unlikely to happen.

Now you've seen the pattern above, use the Socratic Questioning template below to challenge your own intrusive thoughts. You don't need to use all the questions, though they each will help in different ways.

My intrusive thought is . . .	
What evidence is there for this thought?	
What evidence is there against this thought?	
Am I really looking at all the evidence, or only that which supports my thought?	
Am I misinterpreting the evidence?	

Is this thought based on facts? Or is it based on feelings?	
What might other people who know the evidence think? Is it different from my thought?	
Is this a habitual thought I've had before? Why?	
Is this my own thought or did I get it from someone else? If the latter, are they reliable?	
Is this thought a *likely* scenario or is it the *worst-case* scenario?	

If you have given your thoughts and feelings some serious consideration and you still feel like there is an issue in your friendship, you can have a conversation with your friend – as long as you feel safe and able to do so. Having these kinds of conversations in a neutral space and in person is always better than over text message, so that tone is not lost. Start your conversation with 'I feel . . .' statements instead of pointed 'You . . .' statements, so that no one feels attacked. In an ideal friendship, the other person will hear what you have to say and acknowledge why their behaviour has not been good recently, or in the past. Together, you can make a plan to nurture the relationship moving forward.

In more extreme cases, friendships that end negatively can lead to bullying, which has the potential to seriously impact our mental health. If you feel humiliated, abused or embarrassed following interactions with your 'friend', you may want to reconsider the friendship and distance yourself from them.

Of course, friendships can also simply fall apart due to changes in life stages (when your friend becomes a parent but you do not want kids), geography (you move to a different country) and competing demands (your work schedule is too busy). These don't have to mean the end of a friendship, but instead can be nurtured into friendly connection with the right tools. Some common signs of a good friendship include:

- **Open communication:** Telling friends when we're feeling overwhelmed by work and won't have as much time to spend with them.
- **Trust and respect:** Respecting our friends' experiences and trusting them with our own.
- **Consistency:** Making a point to check in and show up regularly, even if it isn't daily or weekly.
- **Quality time and thoughtfulness:** Carving out time to spend with our friends, or sending a card to mark an achievement.
- **Active listening:** Putting our phones down and practising good eye contact when talking with our friends; asking follow-up questions.
- **Positivity:** Sharing enjoyment with one another and celebrating each other's lives.

- **Empathy:** Understanding and appreciating our friends' circumstances when they may be going through a rough time.
- **Boundaries:** Respecting the wishes of our friends when they request time or space, and enforcing our own boundaries when we need to.

Friendships are strengthened and fortified when these principles are practised by both parties.

Love isn't all we need

Romantic relationships are arguably the most turbulent of our interpersonal relationships. They are the reason most of my clients seek therapy. The dating game is a minefield, with a new trend seemingly appearing every month to describe the many ways communication breaks down while courting ('breadcrumbing', 'ghosting' and 'benching', to name just a few).

This section of *Paperback Therapy* could really be a full book. But to keep things simple, below are some core issues you may face in your romantic relationships, and how to deal with them.

- **Communication**: Whether it's radio silence after a first date we thought went well, or the silent treatment following an argument about whose turn it is to turn the dishwasher on, it's easy to notice when there's a communication breakdown in our relationships. It's impossible to know exactly what someone else is feeling, and when their happiness literally depends on us being open and communicative, we should be just that – even if it's a little uncomfortable. If you're not interested in someone, a simple 'Thanks for your time – I don't feel a spark but hope you find what you're looking for' is a respectful way to communicate your feelings. Responding to this message ('Thanks for letting me know'), rather than reacting ('Are you kidding? Why did you make out with me if you felt no spark?!') is a respectful way to reciprocate. Make this easier by counting to three before you answer a triggering question, text or topic – the beat between can enable us to step back and make more informed communication choices.

- **Infidelity**: It doesn't matter whether we've been unfaithful or someone has been unfaithful to us, infidelity is a hard issue to get over in a relationship. But it can happen. We may stray from our current partners because there is something missing in the relationship – time, intimacy, attention and so on. Identifying what it is that is missing is the first step to reconnecting with our romantic partners following infidelity. Trust is a huge part of a relationship, so communicating infidelity – whether acted upon or just a thought – is important. Do so in a neutral environment (not your bedroom or home), in person (instead of over text or email), and with enough time for the conversation to play out (not while waiting for a coffee on your lunch break). Allow enough space and time for the other person to hear and respond to you, knowing this may not all happen in the one sitting. Check in afterwards as to how you're both feeling, and seek third-party mediation if you need support moving forward – together, or apart.
- **Sex and intimacy**: Issues around sex and intimacy can feel incredibly personal, because they relate to moments in which we are at our most vulnerable. These may include having different ideas about how much and what kind of sex is good, when and whether to be monogamous or polyamorous, whether we prefer to fall asleep cuddling or need space to snooze, if public displays of affection are appropriate or not, and issues surrounding sexual performance. When naked, raw and vulnerable in the bedroom, it's hard to have conversations around sex and intimacy. This is why it's sometimes best to approach discontent around these topics in a neutral location that isn't the bedroom. Reiterate what you *do* like about being intimate with your partner, and then approach the subject again, using 'I feel . . .' statements to ensure your partner does not feel attacked.

Award-winning psychosexologist Chantelle Otten says in her book *The Sex Ed You Never Had*: 'Feedback and criticism are different. If you tell your partner that something doesn't feel right and that you would prefer something different, that is just feedback, it's not a criticism. It's a good idea afterwards to talk about how it made you feel and what to do differently next time.'[3] And remember, if someone violates your consent, report it to someone you trust – this is never okay.

- **Abuse and trauma**: Experiencing abuse or trauma at the hands of a romantic partner can be incredibly difficult to deal with, especially when there is also manipulation that makes it hard to see that how we're being treated is wrong. Abuse can be physical or emotional. The former includes hitting, kicking, biting, shoving, and sex without consent. The latter includes neglect, humiliation, control, shaming, dismissing, monitoring, isolating a partner from others, and other acts where a person intentionally says or does things to hurt us. A close friend or a public support person such as a police officer can help you to extricate yourself from an abusive situation, while a therapist can help you to manage feelings of self-worth associated with the trauma. Together with your support system, you can make a plan for avoiding altercations and also plan a safe exit from the relationship. If you don't have a support system available to you, you can phone a 24/7 support service such as 1800RESPECT, MensLine Australia (1300 78 99 78), Lifeline (13 11 14) and more (numbers current at time of printing).
- **Complacency**: It's easy to fall into complacency when in a long-term relationship, where the excitement of the 'honeymoon period' turns into routine. It's at this phase that many of us wonder if the grass is greener in other relationships, especially when fuelled by the unrealistic expectations pop culture presents us with – after all, movies rarely show couples doing the laundry together or paying electricity bills. Along with complacency comes a lack of gratitude, and we can start thinking of our partners as housemates instead of lovers. This can lead to feelings of resentment, or of not being 'seen' and valued. Reignite the spark in your relationship by scheduling regular date nights, using props like Conversation Cards to have conversations outside of your usual topics of interest, and making an effort to compliment one another, often.
- **Attachment**: Our preferred ways of expressing and receiving affection in a relationship are not always the same as those of

our partner. Our partner may wish to spend every day together, while we may relish independence and believe absence makes the heart grow fonder. Our attachment styles are thought to mirror the dynamics we had with our caregivers when we were young children, and include: *secure attachment* – being calm, warm and social, and finding it easy to connect to others; *anxious attachment* – fearing rejection, having low self-esteem and needing constant reassurance; *avoidant attachment* – being independent with high self-esteem, avoiding feelings of intimacy and having difficulty committing; and *fearful-avoidant attachment* (also known as disorganised attachment) – wishing to be loved but finding it difficult to let anyone in due to distrust.[4] Our attachment style can change over time, but it can be handy to try to understand which we may have – and which our partner has – to better understand each other's needs, tendencies and reactions. While someone with an anxious attachment style might need to be reassured that their partner is devoted to them, someone with an avoidant attachment style might react badly to requests for reassurance as it can make them feel trapped or pressured to commit. Being aware of behaviour associated with the different attachment styles can help avoid misunderstandings.

- **Finances**: Money problems can significantly impact relationships. If we have different ideals to our partner around what to spend and what to save, tension can build. This includes hidden financial behaviour, such as gambling without our partner knowing. But money issues don't only come from different belief systems. In fact, with the price of groceries, electricity and water increasing, it's no wonder that the intimate relationships of more than one-third of Australians are impacted by cost-of-living pressures.[5] Having regular and open conversations about finances and expectations around spending money can help mitigate any issues caused by assuming we're all on the same page. Some couples may choose to have regular finance date-nights where they check in on budgets, while others may choose to have a joint account for shared expenses and personal accounts for their own discretionary spending – the goal is to have a plan in place and be transparent with your partner about finances.

- **Arguments**: Fights in relationships can start from small issues, like leaving teabags in the sink, or bigger issues, such as why someone was unfaithful. Regardless of what a fight is about, a swift resolution is the best way to avoid the possibility of it becoming a big blow-up. If you can, take a moment to breathe deeply before responding during an argument. Step away from the situation if you feel you're going to say something you may regret and be sure to circle back to explain how you may have been hurt by something your partner said. It's hard for us to say sorry, but an apology goes a long way when warranted. With that comes forgiveness and the chance to move forward. Our grandparents had it right when they said, 'Don't go to bed angry'. Try to resolve any arguments you can through clear communication (those 'I feel . . .' statements again!) and if you need a third-party mediator for the big ones, seek out a trusted friend or therapist.

- **Incompatibility**: How many children do you want? How often should we spend time with our extended family? Do you mind if I work late again tonight? Do you have the same religious and cultural beliefs as me? How much sex is 'enough' each week? Answering these questions has the potential to reveal incompatibility in a relationship. While they're important questions and we may feel strongly about our own answers, relationships are also built on compromise. Negotiating a compromise on some aspects of our lives is possible through a discussion where both views are shared and both partners are prepared to make sacrifices towards a goal somewhere in the middle. For example, a couple may decide to have extended family dinners fortnightly, to compromise on one's desire to have them weekly, and the other's desire to have them monthly. However, sometimes an agreement just can't be met. When this happens regarding things that are deeply important to us, like having children or where we want to live, we may have to look at the relationship and decide if it truly has a future.

Recognising and working to correct these core issues early on can increase the longevity of your relationship. This is sometimes hard to do, especially when there are third parties like kids or pets involved, which is why many seek therapy (either individually or as a couple). If you're unable to see a therapist, you can try the communication tips in the section on friendship (page 114) to have a conversation about what's hurting you, or you can use the Socratic Questioning exercise above (page 115) to work out whether your thoughts around your relationship are based in fact or feelings.

Family ties

Our family systems are complex, comprising immediate and extended members who ultimately influence one another's behaviour, according to psychiatrist Murray Bowen.[6] Bowen theorised that one family member's needs and abilities can affect all family members, and the relationships each family member has. For instance, how close we are with one particular sibling may impact our relationships with our other siblings, and the way our parents interact with each other often sets the tone for the whole family dynamic. It's not a domino effect, but it is all interconnected.

When a relationship between family members falters, it has the potential to impact the whole unit. Many of the issues that are present in friendships and romantic relationships, such as lack of trust, financial differences, complacency and lack of communication can exist in our relationships with family members. However, while we can choose to connect with friends and romantic partners who have similar values to our own, we don't always have a choice when it comes to family. Your parents or grandparents may have values you consider 'old-fashioned', especially around sex, education or gender roles, while your aunt may have different beliefs about sexuality to you, and your sibling might express views on race that you find distasteful. When these kinds of conflicts arise, there are ways we can try to manage relationships with difficult family members:

- Avoid topics of conflict, such as opinions on upcoming elections or identity
- Ask other family members to be present when we're with the person in question, to act as a 'buffer' by diverting attention

- Limit time spent with those family members who hurt us
- Align with your partner or plus one on an exit strategy at events where the family member will be present
- Set boundaries with the family member, asserting what you will and won't talk about with, or tolerate from, them.

Unfortunately, it's not as easy to move on from family whose values we don't agree with. Sometimes living harmoniously is the best we can do.

When relationships turn sour

Knowing how to resolve conflict is an incredible skill to help build resilience and foster healthier relationships. Regardless of whether the conflict is with a colleague, a friend, a partner, a family member or even an acquaintance, it can fester when left unresolved – the sooner it's mitigated, the better.

Here are some strategies you can use to manage interpersonal conflict:

- Communicate feelings clearly and honestly, and try using the SBI feedback model (see point five on page 134)
- Compromise to meet in the middle
- Reflect on what the other person may be experiencing, by practising empathy
- Forgive each other, where warranted
- Move the conversation forward (don't have the same fight over and over)
- Take a deep breath before responding to any hurtful remarks
- Acknowledge when it may be time to walk away.

If we feel bitter about a person in our life, we should ask ourselves why. Is it really about them as an individual, or is it something they represent? Perhaps they have something we want, or represent a feeling we're seeking. By questioning why it is we feel triggered by a particular person – and thus identifying what may be missing from our lives or what we may be projecting onto others – we can learn more about ourselves. This is known as *shadow work*, whereby we develop self-awareness about traits we may subconsciously reject within ourselves, with a view to accepting our whole self, warts and all. When we love and accept ourselves, we can build stronger bonds with those around us.

Starting over

Sometimes, no matter how much we try to mend a relationship, it just can't be done. Perhaps we feel bullied by a friend or work colleague; perhaps we can no longer look at our lover the same way after discovering a secret of theirs. When it's time to move on from the past and plan for the present, we need to be gentle on ourselves.

First, we need to grieve the loss of the future we're no longer going to have – one with that relationship in it, and any other potential relationships that may stem from ending this one (for more on grieving, see chapter 14). For instance, when ending a relationship with a long-term partner, we may also be ending a future in which we had children with this person, and ending the relationship with the parents-in-law we loved. Acknowledging and grieving the loss of this relationship is an important step in moving forward.

We may to want to put these people out of our minds as much as possible to move on. Deleting or muting them on social media, deleting their number to avoid the late-night text messaging when we are feeling lonely, and asking friends not to mention them to us are all fine boundaries to set if we want to better 'get over' somebody. However, sometimes they will come to mind when we least want them to.

It's also normal to think of particular individuals at big milestone moments in our lives. This sometimes causes concern for people – for example, if they're unable to stop thinking about an ex-boyfriend while planning a wedding with a new partner – but it's very common. If you once imagined a future with a person, it makes sense you will think of them again when that milestone exists in your new future. Acknowledge this with curiosity, and then move on.

When I first got engaged, I couldn't stop thinking about my ex-boyfriend. It made me feel guilty, and question whether I was doing the right thing in marrying my then-fiancé if I couldn't stop thinking about my first love. He would come into my thoughts daily – scary when you're planning your wedding! It wasn't until I spoke to a friend who was also engaged and experiencing the same thing, regularly thinking of her ex-partner, that I realised I wasn't alone. We understood then that this wasn't about our exes at all, it was because we were being reminded of the moments we previously thought we might share with them – the wedding.

Monica, 36
Adelaide, South Australia

The end of a relationship can hurt for a long, long time. Memories of the good times (and the bad) may come in waves, and when we least expect them. Having a strong support system, taking care of ourselves, feeling our feelings and seeking professional help can all assist us to move forward with our lives once a relationship ends.

———

Our relationships are a huge part of our lives, so it's important that they are as healthy as we're able to make them. We've learned in this chapter that the health of an interpersonal relationship is not always in our control; however, we do have the ability to set boundaries and mitigate any negative feelings as best we can. Review the relationships in your life currently, and decide: Are they truly making me happy? If the answer is no, consider what actions you can put into practice from this chapter to improve your relationships and build yourself a stronger social support system.

Chapter 10

Protecting yourself

Setting and maintaining boundaries

While *we* may be doing the best we can to work on our own mental wellbeing, it's likely that not everyone in our lives can say the same. Setting boundaries and communicating our needs within personal and professional relationships helps to build our self-worth and emotional tolerance.

A boundary is a limit that we set between another person and ourselves. It is not a physical 'wall', but it can be helpful to think of it as an invisible fence that surrounds and protects us. A boundary helps us to understand where we end and others begin, and it helps us to know what is ours (our beliefs, needs, emotions, thoughts, physical and emotional spaces) and what is someone else's. Setting boundaries is a skill that many of us learn as we enter adulthood, an acknowledgement that every individual is responsible for themselves.

Our ability to set boundaries successfully is established through learned behaviour, usually as a child. If in childhood we were denied privacy by overprotective parents or – on the flipside – felt constantly unmonitored and able to do whatever we wanted to, we may have difficulty setting boundaries of our own in adulthood. We may feel as though we need to fix others, that we need to always say 'yes' or that we're responsible for other people's feelings. Unlearning these beliefs can be difficult, but it is important to ensure our own emotional regulation.

Burnout is a common symptom we may experience when we have not set boundaries around how we use our energy. It often occurs when we are unable to meet our own needs, instead focusing our energy on meeting other people's. Think of it as having a set amount of energy each day. Without boundaries, we may happily go around giving time and energy to other people in our lives, overextending ourselves and leaving our own energy stores depleted. Setting boundaries helps us to protect energy for ourselves and reduce feelings of burnout, all by simply saying 'no' or 'not right now'.

If we don't value our time or are too generous with our love (yes, there is such a thing!), we teach those around us that our time is not valuable or that we'll always love them, regardless of what they may do to us. Setting boundaries for ourselves and others can improve our self-worth by demonstrating how we value ourselves, and helping to attract people into our lives who see that worth. Honouring our capacity, and only giving what we can, will unlock time for us to rest and recharge.

You may be thinking that you simply like giving gifts, or donating your time, or writing letters to friends, or staying back to work late on projects. And this very well may be true (good on you!). But for many of us, these acts of service and oversharing of energy aren't things we truly want to *do* – they're things we seek validation *from*. It's not the *action*, it's the *reaction* that we value – a worthiness we are desperately trying to prove (instead of it coming from ourselves). This is commonly known as 'people pleasing'.

It's hard to set boundaries as a people pleaser – we don't want to upset other people or be seen as a burden. Nobody wants to be the 'bad guy'. This is where the Power to Control exercise in chapter 2 becomes useful once again, because it can remind us that there are things we cannot control (what other people think of us), things that we can control (our reactions and behaviour), and where our attention should be focused (into the latter).

It is very likely that when we first establish a boundary, especially with someone we love, we may feel uncomfortable. But the hope is that we will sit in this discomfort and also feel strong, because we are choosing to assert ourselves and establish an expectation within that relationship that will take care of our own needs in the long run.

Reminding ourselves of our rights as a human in a relationship – be it a friendship, work relationship or familial one – is a nice way to remember that it's okay to set boundaries if our emotional needs are not being met. American psychologist Edmund J. Bourne drafted a 'Personal Bill of Rights' to help his clients identify twenty-five rights they could assert in their relationships.[1] Read the list below, and highlight the ones you believe to be true:

1. I have the right to ask for what I want.
2. I have the right to say 'no' to requests or demands I can't meet.
3. I have the right to express all of my feelings, positive or negative.
4. I have the right to change my mind.
5. I have the right to make mistakes and not have to be perfect.
6. I have the right to follow my own values and standards.
7. I have the right to say no to anything when I feel I am not ready, it is unsafe, or it violates my values.
8. I have the right to determine my own priorities.
9. I have the right *not* to be responsible for others' behaviour, actions, feelings, or problems.
10. I have the right to expect honesty from others.
11. I have the right to be angry at someone I love.
12. I have the right to be uniquely myself.
13. I have the right to feel scared and say 'I'm afraid'.
14. I have the right to say 'I don't know'.
15. I have the right not to give excuses or reasons for my behaviour.
16. I have the right to make decisions based on my feelings.
17. I have the right to my own needs for personal space and time.
18. I have the right to be playful and frivolous.
19. I have the right to be healthier than those around me.
20. I have the right to be in a non-abusive environment.

21. I have the right to make friends and be comfortable around people.
22. I have the right to change and grow.
23. I have the right to have my needs and wants respected by others.
24. I have the right to be treated with dignity and respect.
25. I have the right to be happy.

Hint: They all should be highlighted. We all have the right to all of the above.

Boundaries in our personal lives

Boundaries can be crossed in many different types of interpersonal relationships. Friends, family members, acquaintances and even people at the grocery store can knowingly and unknowingly impact our mood by doing or saying things that breach our boundaries. While sometimes it's easy to ignore these actions or words, they can be hard to forget when they come from someone we love.

This can be even more difficult in an interpersonal relationship that includes physical closeness. Even if we don't want to see a person because they make us feel awful, we may have to be in the same room as them.

Personal boundaries are the *internal* fences we can establish to manage our emotional safety and wellbeing. *External* boundaries are often difficult to set; however, internal ones are essential to living our best lives. An example of external and internal boundary setting is as follows:

Scenario: Marlowe's cousin Caleb makes them feel uncomfortable every time they see him. Marlowe encounters Caleb at every Christmas, birthday and family celebration, and always feels awful afterwards.
External boundary: Marlowe could *refuse to go* to family events, so they don't have to see their cousin. This is not always possible as Marlowe's wider family expects to see them there, and Marlowe don't mind hanging out with everyone else in the family – it's just Caleb who makes them feel bad.
Internal boundary: Marlowe could *decide not to engage* with their cousin at the family event, instead staying close to another family member they trust. If Caleb tries to engage with Marlowe, they can simply smile and change the subject, or move the conversation to a neutral topic with other family members also involved.

It's best to think of our boundaries ahead of time, so we can reinforce them when they are being crossed. Remember, our internal 'fence' is not only about keeping negative actions and words *out* (this is known as an emotional boundary) – it's also there to keep important things, such as energy, attention and love, *in* where we need them most (this is called a resource boundary).

After a very quick-moving eighteen-month relationship ended, I found myself in a codependent relationship with my ex-partner. Close friends without any boundaries, I thought this was working for us until she got a new partner who was unhappy with us staying friends. After an unsuccessful year of trying to make this person comfortable with me, I made the decision to no longer make myself smaller to fit in their lives. I told my ex-partner this, and she responded by saying she needed space from me.

While tough at first, I believe the boundaries have been ultimately healthy for both of us. The reality of a boundaryless relationship, whether platonic or romantic, is that it becomes mentally and emotionally straining. It comes at the cost of addressing your needs and your mental health – something I feel we both experienced.

Ben, 31
Melbourne, Victoria

Eleven steps to setting boundaries effectively

1. **Choose the time and place to have a conversation about boundaries, one on one**: You want the person's full attention and you want to allow enough time for the conversation to take as long as it takes – this means no squeezing it in over a lunch break.
2. **Choose your method of communication**: In person is always best so that no body-language cues get lost. However, this isn't always

possible, for instance if you live far away or feel unsafe. The next best form of communication is video or phone call, which have the added benefit of allowing you to prepare and read from cue cards if you feel you need them. They can help you stay firm on setting your boundaries.

3. **Know what it is you want to say before you say it**: Having a clear key message that you want to communicate and remembering this will keep you on track. Start with what you need from them and ask politely rather than aggressively. Consider saying 'I need you to please . . .' instead of 'Next time, why don't you just . . .'

4. **Have an ideal outcome in mind**: An end scenario that is a win-win for both of you will help the other person visualise what it is you need from them. Float this scenario with the other person and then ask them what they think. Asking a question like 'How would you feel about phoning me before coming over, so I can make sure I have free time to spend with you?' shows that you are open to working with them, and if they say no, loop back to point three: 'I need you to please . . .'

5. **Be direct and tell the person exactly what you want or don't want from them**: Describe the *situation* where they last crossed your boundaries, the *behaviour* they exhibited when doing so, and the *impact* that had on you. This is known as the SBI feedback model and it is an effective way to stick to the facts when setting your boundaries.[2] For example, 'Last time you came over unexpectedly, I was working on an important project and your visit meant that I didn't have enough time to finish my work and felt very stressed. I need you to please call and ask if I'm free before you drop by.' Don't beat around the bush. The more specific you can be, the more likely it is you will be heard.

6. **Own your feelings by inserting yourself into the language you use**: 'I feel . . . when you . . .' is a lot less confronting to the other person than 'You made me feel . . .'

7. **Prepare for pushback from those you're setting boundaries with**: This is especially important if you are setting boundaries to stop a previously common behaviour and it may come as a shock to the other person. They may not acknowledge your boundaries, or they

may not understand why you're establishing them, and it's important to be prepared to have your new boundaries questioned or challenged. Try to remain calm, and move on to the next step.

8. **Listen to their side of the story and give them time to share it:** They may be unaware they have been crossing your boundaries, or it's possible they may be pushing yours because they feel you are pushing theirs. Entering into the conversation about boundaries with an open mind will ensure a more positive outcome for everyone.

9. **Reiterate your boundaries, often, to yourself and others:** Any time your boundary is crossed, re-establish it with the other person and be firm in your approach. Feel free to use language such as 'As I asked you last time, I need you to . . .'

10. **That being said, don't feel as though you need to overexplain:** If questioned about why you're setting your boundary, simple phrases like 'because it's what I need right now' or 'because I'm focusing on me' can help you respectfully answer the other person while holding firm for yourself.

11. **Remember your 'why':** If you feel your boundaries being pushed by other people, turn inward and remind yourself why you felt it was important to set the boundary in the first place. This could be as simple as remembering 'I am enough', or as tangible as 'because I have a deadline of my own that I need to prioritise.'

My mother would consistently call me to complain about my father, who had left her a few months earlier. I would be in the middle of work and feel guilty about not answering her call, but sometimes I had to decline it because I just didn't have the energy or time to take on her emotions on top of mine – I was also hurting about the divorce.

I finally had to tell her that I was sorry, but I could not be her sounding board anymore. It was unfair for her to talk about my father like that, especially when I was trying to maintain my relationship with him. She was upset and it was a tough conversation, but I was able to explain that I felt she was

> *trying to pit him against me and that I preferred she speak with a professional.*
>
> *It's been years now, and the boundary remains in place. Only occasionally do I need to reassert it, and doing so is easier every time because the foundation for that discussion is already established.*
>
> **Lola, 23**
> **Hobart, Tasmania**

The key to setting boundaries is to focus on providing alternatives, not explanations. Recommend something instead of what is being asked of you, rather than only a rationale as to why you can't/don't want to do what is asked of you. 'No' is a full sentence; we don't need to over-explain our reasons. For instance, you could say 'I can't meet you at seven o'clock tonight for a drink, but how about we meet at five for a coffee?' instead of 'I can't meet you at seven o'clock for a drink because you get mean when you drink alcohol.'

Boundaries in the workplace

It's easy for the boundaries between our personal lives and our professional lives to blur, especially when we share aspects of our personalities online. This is even truer since the usual workplace and education model recently shifted from face-to-face to online, and then to a hybrid one for many of us. When our work set-up is at home and the clock ticks past 5 pm, it's now easier for an employer to say, 'Can you just hop online and check the presentation I sent you?' This is where the ability to set effective boundaries and respectfully say 'no' comes into play.

Each workplace has different management models and employee–employer relationships. This means we need to set boundaries that are unique to our own circumstances and those in our workplace. If we're beginning to feel the symptoms of burnout (decreased satisfaction, lack of motivation, cynicism, helplessness, lethargy, etc.), it's a good time to take a beat and reflect on what our own personal limits could be in the workplace. Writing these down and sharing them with our direct report if we feel comfortable opens the conversation to start working on them together and ensures our boundaries are clearly and respectfully set.

Setting boundaries with your boss can appear more difficult than setting boundaries with a colleague, due to the power dynamic. Saying no can be hard when receiving requests from your boss; however, creating a mentally safe workplace for yourself does not discriminate between role and rank.

It's important to be a team player. Offer alternative solutions where appropriate rather than a blanket refusal of all requests that may cross your boundaries.

Communicating with empathy and understanding towards your boss will ensure you are able to maintain a good professional relationship while still adhering to your own personal limits.

Mechelen D'Souza, registered psychologist

Some professional boundaries to consider setting in the workplace:

- At what times you will check and respond to emails
- How available you will be to your team when you are off the clock
- How long meetings should be, depending on the agenda
- Whether you really need to attend certain meetings, or if you can just get the notes so you can protect your time
- Where you will have meetings – in a closed room, at a cafe, etc; this may differ depending on your level of security with the person or people you are meeting with
- How and where you will engage with a colleague if they are hot-headed or have negative energy
- What kind of relationships and contact you will have with colleagues outside of work
- What deadlines you set and accept from clients and colleagues, and how these might change depending on your workload.

I've learned there is a fine line between having a great work ethic and saying yes to everything to get ahead. It's absolutely okay to want to work hard, to have big career goals, to put effort into something you are passionate about, but now I realise the importance of making sure I leave something in the tank for other areas of my life. It is important for me to find balance, and find aspirations in other areas of my life that I can cultivate and enjoy. In a nutshell, I'm no longer putting all my eggs in one basket.

Andrea, 38
Western Sydney, New South Wales

Exercise: Safe Space

Internal boundaries help to protect you from emotional dysregulation, while external boundaries can help you to create a space in which to feel and acknowledge these emotions.

If you have the means, designate a safe space in your home and/or workplace that can become your sanctuary. This can be a single chair, or an entire room – the important thing is that it is comfortable for you. Choose soft furnishings like blankets and pillows in colours and textures you love. Put soft shoes or socks near the area so you can slide into them when you arrive (and even better, unrestrictive clothing). Establish a sound system that can play music that calms you, even if simply from your phone. Consider the scent of the area: are you able to burn a candle or put a diffuser in the space with a relaxing scent, or one that evokes positive memories? If you like reading, put your favourite feelgood books beside the chair. If you're more into podcasts, set up a playlist of shows that make you laugh (no crime, please).

Whenever you feel the need, sit comfortably in that space, and turn on your music, your sounds, your scent. Sit with your favourite beverage or food of choice in your lap. Bring awareness to your senses while you sit there. What do you notice? What do you see? Feel? Taste? Smell? Hear? This task brings you back into the present and away from your emotions.

Try to stay off technology during this time, too. It's easy to hop from tab to tab and be triggered while unconsciously 'doomscrolling' on social media. This space is not for them. You've set a boundary around yourself. This space is just for you and your thoughts.

Below are some items to consider bringing into your safe space. Add your own to the list.

TOUCH	HEAR	SMELL	TASTE	SEE
Soft blankets	Brown noise	Candles or diffusers	Favourite snacks or sweets	A good book
Slippers or soft socks	Happy podcasts	Fresh flowers		A landscape or garden
Mala beads	Voice notes from a friend	Cooking smells	Tea, coffee or other warm drinks of choice	Photos of loved ones who treat you well
Your cat or dog's fur	A great playlist	The ocean or other nature smells	Chewing gum or mints	
A cosy couch	The ocean or other nature sounds	Fresh coffee grounds		A vision board or guiding mission statement
				New growth on a plant

Hint: Making a safe space in your workplace isn't always possible. If you can't fully remake your area, consider which of the above elements you could add to the space in which you spend the most time. Maybe it's a small plant, a tiny diffuser, a soft blanket or a specific 'Really Good Tunes' playlist that you can turn to when feeling overwhelmed.

When someone doesn't respect our boundaries

We can't change people; however, we can change our boundaries, and our reactions and proximity to others. It's important that we know when to walk away from somebody or something that doesn't serve us. If we have tried to continually assert our boundaries and they are disrespected, it's a sign that we may need to move on.

Don't fall prey to the 'sunk cost fallacy' – the irrational belief that we must continue to do something just because we've invested un-recoverable resources into it in the past. We may have 'sunk' decades of energy into a friendship, years of dedication into our career or hours into family catch-ups, but if our friend, boss or cousin continues to cross our boundaries and make us feel 'less than', it's time to decide if we're ready to walk away for real. Will we ultimately be happier without them, than with the boundary crossing and emotional dysregulation?

> *Pay attention to your emotions and thoughts at work if your boundaries are continuously broken. If a crossing of bound-aries is the culprit for ongoing thoughts or feelings of fatigue, irritability, feeling unheard and more, then your workplace may be mentally unsafe for you. It may be time for you to escalate the concerns to management and, failing that, look for a new working environment where your boundaries will be adhered to.*
>
> **Mechelen D'Souza, registered psychologist**

Boundaries are absolutely vital to maintaining the energy we want to take into the world. Importantly, they are not about cutting people off from our lives, but instead about being assertive and ensuring our needs are being met as best as they can be. By reflecting on the bound-aries we set for ourselves in the workplace and our relationships, we can arm ourselves against external factors that may otherwise be trig-gering. What boundaries are you going to set today?

Chapter 11

Creativity is a wild mind

The arts as therapy

Remember how good it felt to paint on an easel as a child? To conjure an image from your mind and bring it to life through nothing but paint, pencils and paper?

Art itself is expressive, which is why it makes sense to use it as a tool to help recognise and release emotions. Art can help us to communicate, relieve stress by redirecting our focus, bring forward new parts of our personality and (best of all) it can be executed relatively affordably – often with items found around the house.

Modern therapies often use art-based techniques to cross cultural, age-based or cognitive divides. Writing, painting, sculpting, dancing and singing all stem from a language that most of us understand: creativity. These therapies integrate creative processes with therapeutic techniques to resolve problems, relieve stress, improve interpersonal skills, change behaviour and strengthen self-awareness.

Not all of us are able to communicate our feelings, wants or boundaries clearly. Very young people might not yet have a full vocabulary available to them, while older people who struggle with dementia may have a hard time finding the right words. Those who are neurodivergent or whose primary language is different from those around them, as well as those who have suffered trauma, can also find communicating their feelings challenging. These are all examples of situations where arts therapy techniques can help bridge the gap of storytelling, whether that be with other people or simply expressing ourselves.

> *Creativity has no limits, and when reaching into our creative energies, we begin to trust our intuition. That is the magical formula that allows art therapy to direct clients towards the healing process.*
>
> **Bashar Hanna OAM, member of the International Institute for Complementary Therapists**

In 2019, the World Health Organization released a report demonstrating the benefits of the arts on the promotion of mental and physical health.[1] It found the arts could affect the social determinants of health, support child development, encourage health-promoting behaviours, help to prevent ill health and support caregiving. It also found the arts can help people experiencing mental illness, support care for people with acute conditions, help to support people with neurodevelopmental and neurological disorders, assist with the management of noncommunicable diseases and support end-of-life care. Perhaps most importantly, the report acknowledged that the arts play an important role in strengthening structures and ways for collaboration between culture, social care and health sectors.

What is arts therapy?

We don't need to 'know art' to practise the arts as therapy. In fact, it's a very freeing and non-judgemental way to express emotions.

When we produce art of any kind, it almost always contains hidden meaning: metaphors and symbols that help to identify emotions that we may feel but haven't yet named. For instance, when a child paints their family home with a greying sky instead of the typical blue

COMPONENTS
• Aesthetic engagement • Involvement of the imagination • Sensory activation • Evocation of emotion • Cognitive stimulation • Social interaction • Physical activity • Engagement with themes of health • Interaction with healthcare settings

RESPONSES
Psychological • i.e. enhanced self-efficacy, coping and emotional regulation **Physiological** • i.e. lower stress hormone response, enhanced immune function and higher cardiovascular activity **Social** • i.e. reduced loneliness and isolation, enhanced social support and improved social behaviours **Behavioural** • i.e. increased exercise, adaption of healthier behaviours, skills development

OUTCOMES
• Prevention • Promotion • Management • Treatment

Figure 11.1 How the arts link with health, according to the World Health Organization.[2]

sky with a sun in the corner of the page, this may represent fear, sadness or dread surrounding their family life. A therapist might help us to uncover what it is we're feeling about life at home when these anomalies are presented, but even the act of producing art and analysing it for ourselves can benefit our mental health and self-understanding.

Arts therapy isn't just drawing or painting. We can choose to mould characters with Play-Doh or clay; play an instrument to release our emotions; dance interpretively; write poetry and discuss it later with our friends, family or therapist (or not); or participate in other perform-ative arts, such as a puppet show. The important thing is to choose a form of art that appeals to us.

Some examples of creative or arts therapy include:

- **Art therapy**: Using drawing, sculpting, painting and other artistic techniques to interpret feelings and behaviour through non-verbal metaphors and messages.
- **Dance therapy**: Dancing and moving freely, often representing externally an internal challenge.
- **Drama therapy**: Expressing feelings, practising healthy behaviours and interacting with others through theatrical means.
- **Expressive arts therapy**: Listening to and playing music, reading and writing poetry, drawing, journalling, dancing or sculpting to tell life stories, strengthen interpersonal relationships and heal from traumatic experiences.
- **Music therapy**: Creating new music, singing as a group or one on one, or playing instruments; especially good for treating emotions tied to physical pain, influencing mood and reducing anxiety.
- **Play therapy**: Playing with toys or models to understand our needs and solve problems, often without guidelines or rules.

The great thing about arts therapy is that it takes our experience from within and puts it out – onto the page, onto the paper or into the Play-Doh. This externalises the experience, making it easier for us to process.

Our creative brains

The arts work as therapy because they engage creativity and put us into a 'flow state'. Even the simple act of watching someone else be creative can encourage us to gain new insights about 'being' in the world.[3] This is because of creative flow, the state we enter when completely immersed in a task, which causes our brainwaves and our heart rate to slow down and new thoughts to form.[4]

Being in a flow state means being so wholly engrossed in an activity that our brain function changes and our body calms itself, reducing any feelings of anxiety. Once our body is calm, concentrating on the creative task at hand is even more engaging, and the effect doesn't stop once the task is completed. Throughout this process, we become less critical of our ideas and more courageous. In fact, the end result of completing a creative task is similar to reaching any other big goal – we get a boost in dopamine and feel really good – even motivated! That's why it's hard to stop flexing our creative muscles once we start.

Research shows that creativity can serve people from all walks of life. Those with depression or who are isolated can connect with their feelings, culture or community through creative pursuits, while those who experience dementia have been shown to sharpen their senses and reconnect with their personalities through art.[5] Not into creating pictures through painting or drawing? Creative writing can help you to manage negative emotions too, by helping you to overcome trauma or negative experiences.[6]

There are other benefits, too. Meditation, mindfulness and yoga exercises aren't for everybody, but the same benefits can be sought from engaging in creative pursuits, with the brain acting in a very similar way when in flow. Building positive emotion through creativity expands our perspective so that we notice more possibilities in our lives – it literally gives us hope for the future.

The very process of making art requires us to make decisions we might otherwise not make in life, such as which tools to use, where to start and when to finish. Interpreting the end result and figuring out what it all means is part of the process, helping us also with decision fatigue and meaning making.[7]

In a study of more than 1500 CEOs by tech giant IBM, creativity was identified as the most important quality in a leader.[8] In fact, the respondents shared that leaders who engaged their creativity were more inviting of disruptive innovation, considered unusual ways to drastically change their businesses, were more comfortable with ambiguity, and were courageous and visionary enough to make decisions that altered the status quo. Creativity makes us consider alternative ways to solve problems that we may not have explored before – what a great tool to have in life!

Unlocking creativity

Entering the flow state is easily done when we have the right knowhow. Here is what you can do – and avoid – to harness your creativity for better mental wellbeing.

> *I encourage every human to look for the creative side of their inner being, because the moment they discover such a quality, they'll value its effect once their lives start changing and their resilience grows when faced with the challenges of life.*
>
> **Bashar Hanna OAM, member of the International Institute for Complementary Therapists**

MORE OF THIS	LESS OF THIS
Time outdoors: Appreciating nature through the outdoors is a great way to cultivate creativity, especially if you take notice. Give yourself a challenge each time you go outdoors to ensure you really connect, e.g. find twenty purple things in nature, or take photos of five unique spider-web shapes.	**Time constraints**: Limiting your creative time adds external pressure, which you don't need while creating. Try to avoid picking up your paintbrush or pen when you know you need to be somewhere in an hour.
Rituals: Little rituals can get you in the creative 'zone'. Try using the same scented candle and listening to the same playlist each time you create to help you enter flow state more quickly. *Shout out to my 'Lyricless Background' Spotify playlist for helping me enter a flow state while writing this book. Listen for yourself by scanning this QR code:* 	**Rushing**: Your brain needs time to breathe. It's too easy these days to schedule every little minute of your day and rush through life. In fact, the thing no one tells you about being an adult is that the to-do list never ends (clean the house, do the gardening, pay the bills, meet with friends, schedule the doctor's appointment . . .). It's okay to have a full to-do list, but don't get so busy that you forget to press pause and live the life you've created for yourself.
Diversity: Read books written by people from different cultures or backgrounds, or with lived experiences different to your own; spend time with people outside of your friendship group; listen to music from different genres.	**Monotony**: Eat the same lunch, dress in the same outfit, catch the same bus to work each day? Mix things up to add variety and get different synapses in your brain firing and boost your creativity.

MORE OF THIS	LESS OF THIS
Meditation: Hack your way to flow state through meditation, which opens your mind to new ideas and improves attention. Try a guided meditation app or podcast if you're new to the practice.	**Digital connection**: Always being connected, scrolling social media and being bombarded by external messages leaves you little time to listen to the messages from inside. Turn your devices off for an afternoon and get back to basics, using pen and paper.
Free play: Do you remember being a little kid and having free play – a time when there was no goal and no rules except to have fun? Bring back free play in your week as a time for creating, moving or exploring without limitations.	**Passive consumption**: Sometimes, all we want to do is binge Netflix or look at memes, and sometimes that's okay. It can be hard, though, to get in touch with our own originality when we're consuming too much content made by others.
Acceptance: You won't be an amazing painter on day one. Don't let that discourage you. Going into the creative process with the understanding that you'll accept what you produce, without judgement, will make it a much more pleasurable experience.	**Judgement**: Close your ears to judgement – from yourself and others – while you're creating. If you're not yet comfortable showing your art, that's okay – it's for you, after all. And if someone dares to judge it? Dismiss their thoughts – there's no room for them here in your area of self-growth.
Movement: Exercising gets your blood pumping and helps to release endorphins – hormones that reduce pain, relieve stress and help you to feel good. Taking a long walk is also a great way to give yourself time to think and daydream about your creative pursuits.	**Late nights**: Bad sleep hygiene is having a bedtime routine that is unconducive to getting a good night's sleep. Try to improve your sleep hygiene by turning off digital devices an hour before bed, sleeping in clean sheets, wearing an eye mask, using lavender oil and playing white noise to drown out distracting external sounds. A well-rested mind is capable of great creativity.

MORE OF THIS	LESS OF THIS
Curiosity: Be curious about what you create, and what you're instinctively drawn to. For example, why do you like using the colour blue in your art? Does it make you feel calm or remind you of childhood holidays by the seaside?	**Closed-mindedness**: It can be easy to dismiss things we don't agree with or that don't interest us, but when we open our minds to the opinions and interests of others, we may discover new inspiration and challenge our own ideas.
Consumption of art: Go to museums, read magazines, browse graffiti art on the street and take pictures of what inspires you.	**Comparison**: It's great to be inspired by other people and to use the traits you like in their work to try to accomplish good things yourself. Comparison is the nasty flipside of inspiration, though, where you want to be as good as or better than somebody else. Don't fall into this trap; there are no winners when creativity becomes a competition with others.
Brainstorming with friends: Talk about all of the above activities with your friends – or, better yet, experience them together. A walk around the park and to a museum discussing things you're drawn to can spark stronger neural pathways through shared experience.	**Negative self-talk**: What would happen if instead of saying to yourself 'I'm not an artist', you said 'I *am* an artist'? Reduce your negative self-talk and you may surprise yourself.

Your arts therapy toolkit

Being creative simply means having the ability to create something new through the use of our imagination, mind and experiences. While comparing ourselves to our ultra-creative friends, colleagues or family members can lead us to conclude that we are 'not the creative type', the truth is that we all have the ability to create.

Shake the belief that you are not creative from your mind (literally shake your head – get it out!). Being creative isn't about being the best, but it is about having a go. Sometimes the best art is made from mistakes.

Here's your shopping list for a starter arts therapy toolkit. (You don't need it all – start small with what you're drawn to.) It contains some suggestions for tools to help you flex your creative muscles, let go of emotions that might be holding you back, and create something that can be just for your eyes only.

- Coloured pencils
- Water-based paints and brushes
- Jars to wash your brushes in
- Play-Doh in three different colours
- An A3-size art journal
- The musical instrument of your choice (guitar, saxophone, triangle . . .)
- Old newspapers to get messy on
- An old t-shirt to wear as an art smock
- Magazines to cut up and collage
- A playlist of your favourite songs
- A large space to spread out in and fall into a flow state
- Comfortable dance shoes
- A journal for writing poetry in
- A phone to film movies or capture images that inspire you.

The Arts in all their forms – music, visual arts, drama, dance, poetry, digital media – have been essential to keeping us all going during the pandemic. For many people struggling with their mental health, Arts Therapy provides opportunities for help-seeking and engagement that offer something different to traditional talking therapies. It is a mental health promotion activity as well as a therapeutic exercise.[9]

Professor Patrick McGorry, professor of youth mental health at the University of Melbourne, Victoria

Exercise: Creative Therapy

Let's enter the flow state together. Use the creative prompts below and take note of what style of art you most connect with.

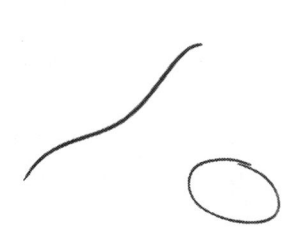

Use this prompt to **DRAW** the first thing that comes to mind when you think of a person you love.

Put on your favourite childhood song and **DANCE** without judgement, flinging your arms about and jumping up high. How do you feel?

Pick up an old newspaper and wet it with a mix of water and glue. **SCULPT** it into a shape that expresses how you feel right now.

Find three items you can use as toys in your home. You're going to **PLAY** with them and create the story of your life.

POWER

Using this word as a prompt, **WRITE** a poem or story that reflects how you wish to present to the world this week.

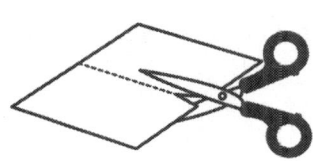

Cut pictures out of old magazines and **CREATE** an image that makes you think happy and positive thoughts.

Narrative therapy

Just as arts therapies help with storytelling, so too does narrative therapy, a style of therapy that understands the human experience, identity and meaning making to be embedded in story.[10] Narrative therapy looks at how we construct the story of our lives, and helps us to separate the story ('narrative') from ourselves to demonstrate that alternative directions for our lives are, in fact, possible.

Narrative therapy was born in the 1980s, created by social workers Michael White and David Epson, and takes a social-constructionist view. In narrative therapy, we listen to the socio-political and cultural inputs that shape our storytelling – whether this is growing up in the time of #MeToo, having Italian heritage, or holding specific religious beliefs – and take notice of how they shape the way we think and speak about ourselves. We then externalise the problem stories that we tell ourselves to change the level of influence they have on us (e.g. 'I am an angry person' becomes 'I am a person who is feeling anger right now'). Once the level of influence has changed, we are better able to manage or change the problem – because it is not ingrained within us.

We can change our beliefs by retelling our stories in more positive ways, shifting from stories that are problem-saturated and oppressive to ones that are enriched (or 'thickened', as White and Epson like to say) with links to hopes and aspirations, or happy memories. By retelling these stories positively and with detail, we can change our self-beliefs. Think of it as learning how to take on '#MainCharacter Energy', where you as the protagonist are courageous and victorious, rather than a victim.

Here's an example of how using narrative therapy techniques can switch a negative belief, or story, about yourself into a positive one.

PROBLEM STORY

Your current belief:
'I've had three romantic relationships in my life and they have all failed.
I've been the one who was dumped, and it's because I'm unlovable.
My father didn't love me, he walked out on me and my mum when
I was just a child, and since then no person has ever really loved me.'

You are intrinsically linking yourself with being 'unlovable'.

EXTERNALISED PROBLEM STORY

Challenging question:
'Would your best friend say you are unlovable?'

Your answer:
'No, that's silly They love me.'

Challenging belief:
'If they love you, then you yourself aren't unlovable.'

You are separating the problem from yourself.

DECONSTRUCTION

Prompt:
'Tell me about your father leaving . . .'

Your current narrative:
'I remember one day I woke up and his bags were packed, and Mum was
crying. He was saying he had to leave because Mum wasn't ever home,
and he had to provide for us all the time. He left and when I asked
Mum why, she said it was because he didn't love me.'

Prompt:
'Did you hear from him again?'

Your current narrative:
'Yes, he would always send cards and I'd see him once a month, but I never felt like he really wanted to see me because each time, Mum would say he was only coming out of obligation and that he didn't love me.'

Challenging question:
'Looking back now, do you think he did love you?'

Your deconstructed belief:
'Well, he did make the effort to continue to see me and to remember my birthday.'

You are starting to deconstruct the belief that your father didn't love you based on facts and prompts about your problem story.

Your reality is challenged; it was created by the stories you previously told yourself, based on the input you were receiving from your mother.

OUTSIDER WITNESS PRACTICES

Your current narrative:
'I have maybe chosen people as partners who were unavailable to me, perhaps because of fear they may leave me first, like Dad did. I mean, one was married, one was here on a working holiday, and the last was about to start a new job where they had to work long shifts.'

Witnessed and reflected summary:
'So you are lovable, when you choose the right people.'

Your enriched alternative story:
'Yes, I could choose people who were present and give those relationships a chance. How scary!'

Witnessed and reflected summary:
'Yes, it could be scary, but what an opportunity for you to share the love you have.'

Your new narrative is enriched through other people (such as a therapist) witnessing and acknowledging your new beliefs.

Your boundaries:
'[Friend], I am going to start choosing people who are
available to me, to test this theory that I'm lovable.'

Your boundaries, witnessed:
'You are the coolest person and you have so much to offer.
I love you so much and I can't wait to hear how this goes!'

**Others listen to your retelling of the alternate story, acknowledging
and strengthening your belief that you are, in fact, lovable.**

ALTERNATIVE STORY

Your new, more positive narrative (belief):
'What happened to me as a kid doesn't define me. I am someone who is
lovable and worthy of being loved, and I'm likely to find the right person
once I start looking for them in the right places.'

**Your presenting problem narrative is now weak, having been
challenged. Your new story has been validated and reiterated,
to strengthen your belief in it.**

The example above demonstrates how we can represent ourselves to
the world (as 'unlovable', for instance) through the stories we tell
ourselves and others, and through the way we hold onto beliefs about
the past, present and future. These stories may not be factually accurate,
and are influenced by sociocultural norms, expectations and assumed
truths. The experiences shared by a person of colour and a Caucasian
Australian will likely differ in their first-person narrative storytelling,
because of the way each individual is influenced by their relationships
and even the people they are telling the story to. First-person narra-
tives are told with selective memory, that is, with the memories that
are most deeply imprinted in our minds. Often this means we 'forget' a
lot of lived experience, which becomes problematic when these narra-
tives influence our identity and actions.

One of the benefits of externalising a problematic belief is that it helps to separate the problem from ourselves. It's a lot easier to accept the fact that we *made* a mistake than that we *are* a mistake.

Creative art therapies enable us to find meaning in our emotions without the rigidity of some other talk therapy practises. This is why they can also be fun! If you're not yet ready to externalise your emotions or pay for an art therapy kit, consider doodling on your notepads at work or school. It can be interesting to see what flows from your heart through to the pen – and then be curious about why you drew what you did, afterwards.

Chapter 12

Just one more time

Conquering unhealthy habits and addictions

What is the difference between liking a glass of wine or two after a hard day at work and being addicted to alcohol? How about the difference between not finding time to eat and having an eating disorder? Or between smoking a joint to manage pain from a chronic illness and having a drug problem?

The line between an unhealthy habit and having what society calls addiction is blurry, sometimes depending on who you ask. What is considered a simple bad habit for some people may be considered too much for others, and that's okay – until it's not.

Bad habits and why we have them

Most of us can easily identify our own bad habits. They're the little actions or behaviours we do regularly that negatively impact our everyday life. Whether it's staying up late doomscrolling or watching Netflix, spending all our pay each week instead of putting some cash away for a rainy day, putting off for tomorrow that which we could do today, consistently running late for work because we hit snooze on the alarm, or visiting the office snack table more than makes us comfortable, there are many bad habits we experience – and many ways we can work to overcome them.

Knowing why we have a habit (good or bad!) is the key to understanding how we can change the ones that aren't serving us. There are many reasons habits may develop, but generally, our unhealthy habits exist to numb emotions we don't want to experience. We may eat unhealthily because we want to feel better (even for a little bit), or we may hit snooze because we dread going to work in the morning. Until we uncover the 'why' of our actions, conquering them may feel difficult.

Brené Brown writes about why we can't selectively numb emotions in her *New York Times* bestseller, *Dare to Lead*. Numbing emotions takes away the light and shade that is living. We don't want to do this, but we do want to make all colours of life more bearable.

Knowing the emotions we are hoping to dull through unhealthy habits helps us also unlock our triggers. For instance, if we repeatedly procrastinate to reduce feelings of stress, we may be in denial about the length of our to-do list. The physical, A4-sized to-do list is overwhelming and could be a trigger for stress. So what else could we do to reduce that trigger, manage feelings and thus work on our bad habit?

Exercise: Identifying Triggers

Avoiding triggers that increase the likelihood of negative repetitive behaviour helps to mitigate the risk of that behaviour occurring. By identifying and acknowledging the people, places or things that make you want to do something that's not constructive, you can put strategies in place to avoid them. These strategies are also known as 'protective behaviours', and are actions you take to ensure triggers have less of an impact or do not occur at all.

Let's put this into practice:

I most feel like_____
(the negative behaviour, e.g. procrastinating):

* when I am around: _____
  (people, e.g. Juliette, who finishes her work so fast)

* when I am at:_____
  (places, e.g. working from home, where there are other things I could
  do)

* when I am around: _____
  (things, e.g. my huge to-do list, with more things still to do than things
  I've crossed off)

Making a list of how we can deal with our triggers, such as by noting
what we can do instead, can help identify how to manage a risky situation
in the moment:

To reduce the temptation to _____
(negative behaviour, e.g. procrastinate):

* when I am around: _____
  (people, e.g. Juliette), I will: _____

  _____

  (protective behaviour, e.g. pop on my headphones to block out the
  noise of Juliette crossing items off her list)

* when I am at:_____
  (place, e.g. working from home), I will: _____

  _____

  (protective behaviour, e.g. block out time to do the washing instead of
  doing it when I should be working)

- when I am around: _____
  (things, e.g. my huge to-do list), I will: _____

  _____

  _____

  (protective behaviour, e.g. also have a smaller notepad where the urgent actions can live, and all others will be out of sight in the big list)

The best thing about identifying our unhealthy habits is that we can then make a plan to change them. We can avoid tempting situations, but what else could we do to make conquering bad habits easy? A simple mnemonic to remember is 'PURR' (I like to think about being calm and in control, like a cat):

- **Prepare**: If you're unable to avoid triggers, you can try to prepare in advance how you might deal with the tempting situation. For instance, you might tell a friend to text you at 10 pm on a night your partner is away, to remind you to stop scrolling and go to bed.
- **Unite**: Speaking of friends, enlisting support is a wonderful way to help change behaviour – after all, it's much easier to achieve something when you don't feel you're going it alone. Tell your friends, family and colleagues what you're hoping to avoid, and ask that they remind you of your goals when they see you being tempted.
- **Replace**: Sometimes temptation is so prevalent that it's hard to eliminate your bad habit altogether. In this instance, you could replace your habit with something healthier. For instance, perhaps you want to stop eating a block of chocolate every night after dinner, but that sweet craving is intense after you've finished your main meal. You could swap out the chocolate for a healthier sweet snack, like a date filled with peanut butter or a warm cocoa.
- **Reward**: Positive reinforcement is a wonderful way to drive change. Reward yourself for steps you take towards changing your habits. For example, you could book an appointment for a professional manicure after two weeks of not biting your nails. This gives you a

shorter and more achievable timeline to aim for – 'to not bite my nails for fourteen days' is a lot more concrete than 'to stop biting my nails forever' – and it will also demonstrate the long-term reward of continuing your changed behaviour, by showing how your nails could look when polished and manicured.

Why people become addicted

Of course, when unhealthy habits cannot be stopped – and when we have cravings to the point that they are all we think about – it may be a sign there's something more troubling at play.

The difference between a bad habit and an addiction can come down to the will and the ability to stop when we want to. If we promise ourselves that 'this one will be the last one', but we're not truly sure that we could cease the behaviour, we could be experiencing addiction.

Addiction is categorised as a chronic disorder of the brain, caused by a malfunction with reward, motivation and memory. People with an addiction obsessively pursue the feeling of 'reward' that comes with satisfying a craving for certain compulsive behaviour, despite the negative impact on emotional, physical, financial or psychosocial wellbeing.

We can be addicted to all kinds of things – alcohol, food, sex, gambling, drugs, pornography, video games, shopping, the internet and social media, tobacco, exercise, plastic surgery, caffeine and more! For the purposes of this chapter, the focus will be on Australia's more prevalent substance addictions – alcohol and illicit drugs. Regardless of what a person is addicted to, though, the patterns of behaviour and feelings experienced are similar. Here's an example based on illicit drug use:

- Christie first tries cocaine at a party, when a friend asks her if she wants a line. Her brain releases a surge of dopamine as a reward, making her feel good.
- Christie's dopamine levels drop after that first hit wears off. Her brain starts craving that reward once more.
- At a party the next weekend, Christie befriends someone else who offers her cocaine, and she achieves that euphorically good feeling. It's just not quite how she remembers it, though. So, she has a bit more.

- Christie's brain gets used to the good feeling, as she continues to use at parties and events. It gets harder and harder to feel *as good* each time she has cocaine, though. So, she increases the quantity.
- The good feelings continue to come now, but not as easily. And now Christie is also experiencing negative feelings, because the drop down from her good 'high' is much steeper.
- Eventually, Christie starts needing a larger dose of cocaine, more frequently, to simply feel baseline okay in the morning. She can never again get that first extreme 'feel good' high, despite chasing it through months and months of use. And so, the addictive cycle continues.

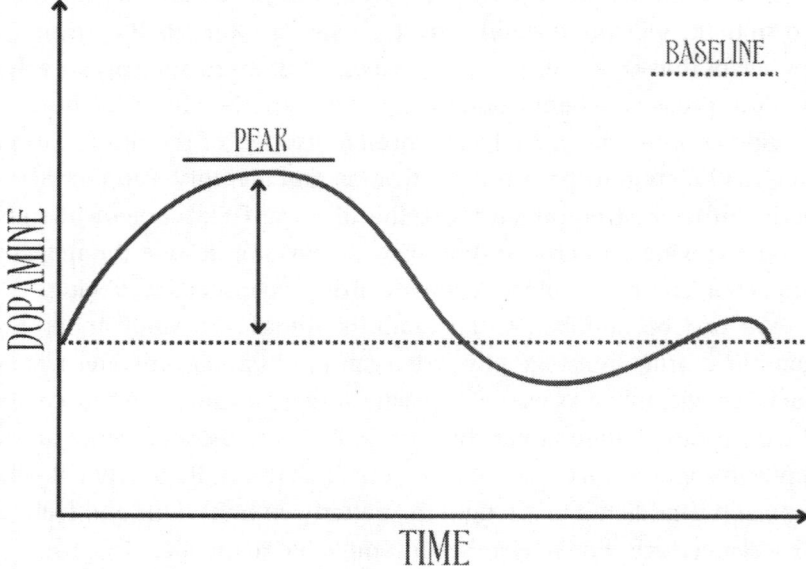

Figure 12.1 Graph showing dopamine surge following substance use. The baseline level of dopamine differs between person to person. The higher the peak, the more dopamine is released.

Most addictive behaviours have two similar characteristics. The first is that they are 'compulsive', in that the desire to satisfy the craving pre-occupies our mind. When will we next satisfy the craving? Where and how will we be able to satisfy it? Who can help us satisfy it? This has potential to damage our interpersonal relationships and jeopardise our employment, as our mind is focused more on the craving than any other commitments. The second characteristic of addictive behaviours is that they are 'problematic' in the sense that satisfying the craving has negative impacts on our wellbeing, relationships, work, finances or social life. For example, we may spend our whole pay cheque on gambling or purchasing drugs, and not be able to afford rent. Or we may drink to excess at a work party and damage our professional relationships by embarrassing ourselves.

Understanding and treating the emotional pain that we hope to dull by using substances can help us to get to the root of the problem. In this way, we are treating the cause (e.g. trauma, anxiety, or grief) while also working on the symptoms (e.g. depression, anger) and the side effects (e.g. denial, guilt) of addiction. Uncovering the underlying cause of an addiction can be daunting if approached alone, and it's always best to approach this with the support of a professional.

Answering these questions can help uncover if you might have a problem with substance misuse:

- Can you guarantee your behaviour when you drink or take drugs? Are you sure you will be responsible for your actions?
- Do you have blackouts when drinking or taking drugs? Are there times when you can't remember parts of a night due to substance use?
- Has your drinking or drug use caused issues in the past? Are there people in your life who are hurt by or ashamed of your substance use?
- Do you envy people who can drink or take drugs without getting into trouble? Why do you envy them – are you not able to avoid trouble yourself?
- Have people around you ever expressed concern about your drinking or drug use?
- Can you picture your life without alcohol or drugs? Why or why not?

Alcohol and other drugs in Australia

One in twenty Australians has a substance use disorder.[1] These disorders can lead to a risk of mental illness and poor health outcomes in the

long term, as well as accidents, violent behaviour, interpersonal relationship issues and mood disorders in the short term. Alcohol is our
most common addiction, with one in six Australians drinking at overall
'risky' levels, followed by smoking, which is practised daily by one in
ten Aussies over the age of fourteen. Illegal drug use is our third most
common addiction, causing more than 1,500 deaths per year.[2]

In a culture that largely celebrates socialising through 'grabbing
a beer', managing consumption of alcohol and other drugs can be
more difficult for some of us than others. Alcohol use is higher among
some demographics including males, younger people, gender-diverse
people, some culturally and linguistically diverse communities, and
those who live in regional areas.[3] Whether substance use turns into a
dependency is not predetermined, and can happen for anyone who
relies more and more on substances to manage mental or physical pain.

Our level of dependency can be identified by a healthcare professional via physical observation and a conversation with us and/or
our family. There are also standardised questionnaires to screen for
unhealthy substance use, such as the Alcohol Use Disorders Identification Test (AUDIT) or the Alcohol, Smoking and Substance Involvement
Screening Test (ASSIST), developed by the World Health Organization.[4]
Both contain questions that refer to substance consumption, potential
dependency and substance-related problems, including concerns that
may be expressed by loved ones.

When an addiction takes over, our self-esteem – how we value and
perceive ourselves – can be severely impacted. In addition, low self-
esteem can increase our tendency to use substances in the first place.
You can see how it could perpetuate a negative cycle. Self-esteem
comes from within but it can be impacted by other people's actions
towards us. If we are treated poorly, bullied or abused by someone close
to us, we may start to believe we are not worthy of happiness. Low self-
esteem can impact our quality of life, increasing the tendency to turn to
a substance or other forms of addiction to feel better about ourselves.
Negative self-worth, perfectionism, fear of trying new things, low self-
care or resilience, self-harm and tolerating poor behaviour from other
people are all too common in people with substance use issues.

When our self-esteem is particularly low, it's easy to believe everything is the worst and that everyone is out to get us, which can cause us to repeat unhealthy behaviours. Even though we may experience some wonderful things in life, low self-esteem can act as a blinder and focus us in on the bad stuff, which can make us spiral into self-pity and substance misuse. This is where gratitude can come in.

Exercise: Gratitude List

Gratitude helps people to remember that not everything is the worst. Making note of the good things – no matter how small – pivots your mindset and can encourage you to be optimistic and look forward to the future.

Create a list of things you're grateful for, and keep a copy of it close by so you can refer to it when you need a reminder of the good in the world – and yourself.

I AM GRATEFUL FOR . . .	BECAUSE . . .
e.g. The weather today	It meant I could go outside and play basketball at the park.
e.g. My friend Primrose	She always makes me laugh, even when I'm feeling down.

If you're struggling to get started, below are twenty examples of things someone might be grateful for:

- My sense of humour
- My job
- Mum and Dad
- My good jeans
- My delicious dinner last night
- *The Office* reruns
- My mentor
- My partner
- My education
- My cat

- How I express myself
- My sex life
- My creativity
- My intelligence
- Nature
- The park down the road
- My comfy bed
- Having Medicare access
- My good grades
- Having a home to be safe within.

Gratitude can also be *a state we are constantly in*, rather than simply *an action we take* here and there. Being perpetually grateful throughout life helps us to feel confident that the rainbow will come after the rain, whereas seeking gratitude only when we feel we need it – though better than nothing – can have a destabilising effect on wellbeing. Consistent practice makes being grateful (and thus, more positive) our default state of being.

When family and friends are affected

For family and friends who love us, watching an addiction slowly take over our lives can be incredibly painful. The lying and self-destructive behaviour we exhibit through substance misuse and other forms of addiction can make those we love anxious, sad and angry. Often, they will long for the way things used to be and may walk on eggshells around us. No matter how much we feel we are hiding our addiction from those we love, our family and friends may know something is up and will want us to seek support.

My partner's alcoholism made me feel isolated, like I was cut off from them. But also, it made me feel like I couldn't help. Suddenly we weren't a team anymore – there was an external thing that wasn't a part of us in our relationship, severing our connection. I always had to consider the addiction before I spoke or lived. They are currently seeking help, but we are far from the journey's end.

Catherine, 38
Sydney, New South Wales

The holidays can be an especially hard time for people experiencing addiction. Moments of celebration like Christmas, Eid al-Fitr, Easter or Pascha can bring forward many triggers, such as financial stress ('I need to buy my family presents'), family conflict ('Uncle Jerry, who I don't get along with, is coming to lunch') and even the presence of addictive substances ('Everyone else is celebrating over a beer'), while other key dates such as anniversaries, school holidays and even changes in seasons can all activate external triggers that increase the likelihood of relapse. It's important, then, to ensure we have the right supports around us.

Telling someone we are struggling with an addiction is the first step towards getting better. This doesn't have to be our partner or friend, though there is a huge benefit to having someone we love as our emotional support through the rough patches – they will almost always be there for us (provided our behaviour doesn't push them away) and we have an established relationship with them so they will know when our behaviour changes and when we may be at risk of relapse. However, it's important to ensure that our supporters are emotionally strong enough to be there for us and that we are leaning on them as part of our wider professional support team. Therapists, doctors, social workers, religious leaders, rehab facilitators and other community leaders can all support us in managing an addiction that is otherwise out of control.

Managing addiction

Admitting we have a problem and seeking support are the first steps to managing an addiction. By admitting that we have a secret that has been eating away at us and negatively impacting our lives, we no longer solely hold the burden. Instead, we can feel empowered to reduce the hold it has on us, and remove the fear that surrounds our addiction (and the fear of who we may become when it's gone).

Peer interventions, such as group therapy, can be incredibly beneficial to those with an addiction. When we're in the cycle of addiction, we tend to believe we are the only person on the Earth going through that very scenario. Coming together in a group challenges this belief, as other people share similar stories of times they experienced feelings and actions like our own.

Group work sees a range of people at various stages of addiction congregate in person and share recent experiences. Attendees share what has been difficult, moments of gratitude and stories of when they were at their lowest low, so that others in the room can see that they are not alone in their addiction – many people have experienced and gotten through to the other side of very similar moments in their lives. Groups are usually managed by a facilitator with lived experience or who has had thorough training in counselling people with specific addiction issues, known as an 'alcohol and other drug' or an 'AOD' counsellor.

By attending a safe space to meet and share stories, we can self-identify our capacity and motivation to change.

Addiction to substances such as drugs and alcohol can be very hard to overcome, especially alone. Alongside group therapy, relapse prevention can include sponsorship, one-to-one talk therapy, pharmacotherapies (medication), rehabilitation visits, hospitalisation to manage symptoms of withdrawal, and more.

The opposite of addiction is connection. Addiction is incredibly lonely, where you have a secretive life because of the shame associated with the addiction. In a group, you realise you're not the only one, you're not alone in this. People who seek support through group interventions start thinking about others and taking their mind outside of just themselves. Whether it's serving others in the group through telling a story about their own journey, or even just bringing the milk for the coffee, the relationships and routines established through group therapy helps to negate the constant inner-thinking addicts often experience.

**Mark Henson, group facilitator, gambling and
AOD counsellor, Oakdene House Foundation**

For a person struggling with negative repetitive behaviours, the temptation to relapse will always be there. Even after several months or years in remission, the risk of relapse remains very real. Reducing unwelcome surprises in life can help mitigate this risk, but this isn't always in our control.

Having a routine can help, though. Routines help us to feel less stress about the tasks ahead, reduce anxiety and avoid choice paralysis ('I've got so much to do, I don't know where to start!'). Guarding against nasty surprises that may trigger a relapse, routines can help give our lives more meaning and purpose. A routine doesn't need to be structured down to the minute, but it should include things we wish to – and can realistically – accomplish each day. Calling a sponsor or supportive friend, eating a healthy breakfast, going to the gym, journalling for twenty minutes, going to therapy, going to bed before 10 pm . . . these could all form part of a routine to help manage an addiction.

Exercise: Daily Routine

Routine helps to foster motivation and focus, which is especially important when we're in the throes of a bad habit. In fact, the simple act of checking a task off a list gives your brain a micro-hit of dopamine, that all-important feelgood chemical. Other ways you can get a dopamine hit include creating something, exercising, listening to music you enjoy, or getting a streak going – such as reading several chapters of a book, running every day, or following your routine for multiple days in a row.

Create your daily routine – and tap into dopamine healthily – by using the table below.

DAILY TASKS	Mon	Tue	Wed	Thu	Fri	Sat	Sun
e.g. Make a healthy breakfast	✓	✓	✓	✓	✓		
e.g. Walk the dog		✓		✓		✓	
e.g. Journal at the café			✓				✓

Supplementing group work with one-on-one sessions with a therapist can help those of us with an addiction to dive deeper into the pain that may be the root cause of excessive substance use. While the topics of loneliness, shame and guilt may be discussed in the group setting, therapists are trained to bring forward what is *causing* these feelings and actions, and support us on our journey to manage addiction. Having someone who doesn't know us personally and who we can share any unresolved trauma with can be empowering. Therapy enables us to say out loud, sometimes for the first time, what it is we are dealing with when facing an addiction. And because it's one on one, the fear of judgement that may come from sharing our stories with family or in the group setting is lessened.

When we are aware of the impact our negative repetitive behaviour has on our lives (financially, emotionally, physically) but are still unwilling to change or seek treatment, this is known as *ambivalence*. Being ambivalent can impact our desire to change, keeping us 'stuck' in unhelpful behaviour. The key to successfully getting a hold on unhelpful behaviour is to clearly identify the benefits of changing, while also acknowledging the downsides that may come with that change – being realistic about what we may gain and lose.

Exercise: Reviewing Ambivalence

Explore your own ambivalence to an unhealthy behaviour with this chart. Whatever you enter in the far left-hand side is likely to trigger relapse. For instance, you may want to numb emotional pain, so you continue to drink more than you should. Consider other ways that you can manage the triggers that you have written on the far right-hand side (e.g. the intrusive thoughts) instead of relapsing. For instance, could you try cognitive behaviour therapy to manage your thoughts instead of reaching for the bottle? The more you work on the two right-hand columns, the more likely you will reduce your ambivalence to change, ensuring you can – and want to – make better choices.

CONTINUE ADDICTIVE BEHAVIOUR		STOP ADDICTIVE BEHAVIOUR	
Positives when continuing addictive behaviour	Negatives when continuing addictive behaviour	Positives when not doing addictive behaviour	Negatives when not doing addictive behaviour
e.g. It numbs the pain I feel	e.g. My family doesn't speak to me	e.g. More money in the bank	e.g. The intrusive thoughts are too much

Whether it's a bad habit like nail biting or doom-scrolling, or a more serious addiction to an illegal substance or to gambling, there are ways to mitigate the impact these habits can have on our lives. By identifying which stage of change we're in and seeking the support of others, we can transform our lives to reduce unproductive or harmful behaviour. It won't happen overnight, but with persistence it is possible to overcome even our worst habits and addictions. And remember, you don't have to fight unhealthy habits on your own – letting someone you trust know that you are struggling is an important first step, and for more serious addiction issues there are a range of professional support options available (find out more in chapter 17).

When you're in the cycle of addiction, you can go years with no connection to anyone else. We're meant to be social beings, and addiction is such a lonely place. When you're deep in it, you're antisocial – there's nothing social about how you live or use as an addict, just lots of secrets and shame. Facilitated groups bring a natural high from the connection with others and the opportunity to bear witness to others doing well on their journey.

Mark Henson, group facilitator, gambling and AOD counsellor, Oakdene House Foundation

Chapter 13

But what if?

Managing worry, stress and anxiety

Life today is pretty chaotic. We are always 'on' and overstimulated, getting alerts through our phones, cars, televisions, computers and even our watches. The world feels smaller than ever, with time zones blurred through social media and 24/7 global news cycles. Plus, our hybrid work environments make traditional work/home boundaries a little blurred. It's no wonder that this leaves us all a little frazzled.

What is stress?

Stress is a state of worry, triggered by a difficult situation that we may not have control over. We all experience stress to some degree, though our tolerance for stress and how we deal with it differs from person to person. The key is to be able to regulate our stress levels and deal with what life throws at us without becoming overwhelmed.

Stressful periods in life include those times when we have extra responsibilities that feel 'just too much', when we don't have enough work to pay our small business bills, when we don't have control over the outcome of a situation (especially if we really like control), when we feel under pressure from other people or because of our financial situation, when we face big changes or decisions, and more.

Ironically, these days we can also become worried about our stress levels! In some cases, this is good – it means we're looking inwards to see how our stress may be impacting us. On the other hand, it's a self-perpetuating cycle that can lead to increased worry and anxiety.

Differentiating healthy stress from unhealthy stress can help us to prevent a decline in our mental wellbeing. Think of healthy stress as the kind that fuels our productivity. It's that adrenaline in our bodies that forces us to work a little harder at the task at hand, to finish on time and do a better job than we might if we were completely calm. On the other hand, unhealthy stress pauses productivity. It can push us into a state of fight, flight, freeze or fawn, and can actually move us away from the task at hand.

- **Fight**: Lashing out and aggressively approaching the perceived stressor. Signs include crying in anger, grinding our teeth, feeling the need to kick or punch, feeling a burning sensation in the tummy, having a tight jaw.
- **Flight**: Running away from the perceived stressor. Signs include excessively exercising, fidgeting and feeling restless, having trouble concentrating, and feeling numbness in our extremities.
- **Freeze**: Feeling unable to move or act against the perceived stressor. Signs include feeling stiff, heavy and cold; feeling dread; and having a slow or loud heartbeat.
- **Fawn**: Attempting to people-please in order to avoid stressful conflict. Signs include being overly agreeable or helpful, and going out of our way to please others.

Once we know how to identify what kind of stress response we're experiencing, we can harness or release it to enable better productivity. For instance, we could optimise the lead time ahead of a project delivery date by knowing the length of time where we feel stressed and driven enough to produce our best work. The project may be due on the 31st, but if we know our stress sweet spot is five days before submitting, we might choose not start the project until the 26th, ensuring we work productively rather than procrastinating over a longer period.

We can also release unhealthy stress by using techniques such as the RAIN Process.

Exercise: RAIN Process

When you're experiencing unhelpful repetitive thoughts, a mnemonic – a pattern of letters that assists in remembering something – can come in handy.

The RAIN Process can help you to feel your emotions without becoming them, putting a stop to the overwhelming feeling of losing control when emotionally overwhelmed. The exercise helps you to take a beat and be with your emotions instead of running from or fighting them. There are several different versions of RAIN that therapists use within their wider mindfulness studies; the version below was initially used by Buddhist teacher Michele McDonald as a meditation technique.

- **R – Recognition**: Recognise that you are experiencing something, and let yourself observe rather than react to this experience. This helps you to develop a better understanding of yourself.

  'I feel like I shouldn't be here. Someone is going to find out I'm a fraud.'

- **A – Acceptance**: Accept what you're feeling. Be with the emotion without trying to change it. This can be uncomfortable, but gets easier the more you practise the RAIN Process.

  'Okay, I understand I am feeling like an imposter. I've felt this way before.'

- **I – Investigation**: Investigate with kindness and curiosity: where are these emotions coming from? Again, this will help you to understand your patterns and start to separate the emotions from your own self.

  'Why am I feeling like an imposter? It's because I'm trying something new in front of a big group of people I admire. It's okay that I feel this way, but I've presented to big groups before and been fine. I can do this.'

- **N – Non-identification**: Have your feeling without becoming it. Detangle the feeling from your identity. A nice way to do this is to say out loud, 'I am feeling anger now, but I am not an angry person', or 'I am feeling sad now, but I am not a sad person', or 'I am feeling worry now, but I am not a worrier'. This compassionately puts the focus on the *feeling* instead of *you*.

  'I feel nervous and like an imposter currently, but I am not a nervous person. I belong here and can do this well.'

Use the following template to support you to work through the RAIN Process. Write down what you Recognise, Accept and Investigate, and a phrase that helps you with Non-Identification.

R

A

I

N

Another way to manage stress is to ensure we get enough sleep. Treating ourselves as we would a newborn baby before bed is a nice way to ensure a relaxing journey towards sleep – turn off screens and wind down with a book, have a bath with a lavender scent, drink something warm before resting, wear soft clothing and swaddle yourself in a warm blanket, listen to white noise or make a quiet space for sleeping, and ensure the room is temperature controlled.

Sometimes, though, getting ourselves off to sleep can be a stressful process in itself! If you're having trouble falling asleep, give this Progressive Muscle Relaxation exercise a go – it can help your body and mind wind down for rest.

Exercise: Progressive Muscle Relaxation

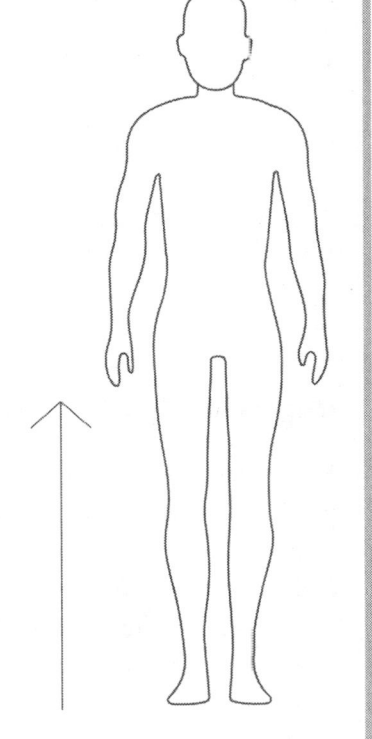

When you're stressed or anxious, your muscles can tense up and become tight. This is why the saying 'Relax your jaw' resonates with so many – because people sometimes hold their feelings in clenched teeth.

This exercise will take you through simple steps to relax your muscles, one by one, in a way that also brings your awareness back into your own body and to the present. Used to regulate your emotions and shut off a racing mind, Progressive Muscle Relaxation can be a great tool to help you to fall asleep.

- Start seated or lying down, in comfortable clothing if possible. Remember to take your time; this is not a race.
- Become aware of how each of your toes feels. Are they rested or are they tight? Give them a little wiggle until they relax.

- Move up to your ankles. Do they feel stuck or loose? Shake them out until they relax. Start with the left one, then move to the right.
- How about your calves? Concentrate on relaxing them too. You can do this by tensing them tight, and then releasing, as often as you need.
- Continue this pattern, moving up your body. Relax your knees, your thighs, your glutes, your genitals, your lower tummy.
- Take a deep breath in and out when you get to your chest, so you can stretch and release your rib cage.
- When you get to your arms, do the left first, and then the right. Wiggle each finger, stretching them out until they feel loose.
- Turn your neck from side to side, up and down, until it stretches and sits comfortably on your shoulders. Most of our tension is kept in the head and neck, so take your time with this part.
- Open your mouth as wide as you can, stretching and then relaxing your jaw. Once it's unclenched, sit with your tongue resting softly at the top of your mouth.
- Slowly move your eyes under their lids from side to side, up and down, and around in circles. You should not feel like you're frowning when your eyes are closed and relaxed.

If you get to the top of your head and are still feeling stressed, start again from the tips of your toes. Practice makes perfect.

Imposter syndrome

Most prevalent in the workplace, imposter syndrome is a manifestation of stress that can also appear in social contexts. Imposter syndrome is when we don't believe we belong in a particular setting, even when we have very much earned our place there. Essentially, we feel like a fraud and project catastrophic thinking. For instance, you may be promoted into a management role but think your junior team members are better at their jobs than you are, and that you'll soon be found out and demoted. Or you may spend an unusual amount of time trying to prove you belong by dressing or acting in accordance with a new social group in school, or according to your preferred gender identity, but you worry people will see through you and question your belonging. In these scenarios, the fear of being found out (the 'what if?') can bring about symptoms such as anxiety, panic, burnout (while we work to prove ourselves), difficulty sleeping and difficulty breathing.

My traumatic childhood and issues with my mother were the seed of my imposter syndrome. Despite growing in confidence as I hit my teenage years and having a popular group of friends, I still never felt good enough at times. That is because deep down I felt that if my own mother couldn't love and protect me, what was wrong with me? It caused me to question myself all of the time, strive for perfection and ultimately showed up as imposter syndrome in my early twenties.

During my first full-time job, my boss publicly berated and humiliated me in a big meeting in front of my peers. It triggered those feelings of 'I am not good enough to be here', 'I have no value to add'. Imposter syndrome can be triggered in perceived good experiences or in bad experiences like bullying, as happened to me.

In 2013, I had a severe panic attack at work caused by my own imposter syndrome. I will never forget that moment. It was terrifying. I couldn't control my breathing, I was sweating, the walls were closing in on me, and everything was just spinning. I thought I was losing my mind. That episode was the catalyst to seek help, to go on the hunt for information to work out what was happening to me. That's when I found out what I had been experiencing had a name, and for the past ten years I've turned overcoming my greatest fear into my expertise.

Alison, 40
Sydney, New South Wales

Imposter syndrome is linked to an excessive need for approval, a trait commonly found in those with anxiety disorders. Being overly concerned with the approval of others can negatively impact our feelings of self-worth, and cause us to seek external validation. We cannot control others' feelings towards us, and so it is a dangerous merry-go-round to constantly chase the approval of other people instead of looking within. The feeling that we are not good enough is linked to a fear of disapproval, often reducing our ability to be assertive in situations that require it – such as moments of confrontation where we need to stand up for ourselves. In fact, people with anxiety disorders tend to try their hardest not to put themselves in confrontational scenarios because of the fear of rejection. We may fail to advocate for a promotion, ask a person out on a date or speak up in a meeting, believing that it's better to not try than to be rejected. When so much good comes from taking chances, can you see how imposter syndrome, stress and anxiety can have a negative impact on our engagement with life?

Anxiety disorders

A quickening pulse, feelings of nervousness, blurry vision, difficulty focusing or sleeping, irritability, tightness in your chest, and tense muscles in your jaw or neck are all symptoms of stress. However, when these are continual and feel overwhelming more often than not, it may be the sign of an anxiety disorder. Anxiety disorders are the most prevalent mental health condition in Australia, impacting 3.3 million people.[1] Because of the way these manifest – developing over time, sometimes from stress – it can be hard to know exactly when we should seek support.

Anxiety disorders may be triggered by unresolved trauma or shame, especially if these are experienced at a young age. Given that people with anxiety disorders have a seemingly constant perception that something bad like shame, loss, failure or injury might occur, it makes sense that if we've experienced this previously, we believe it may happen again. Past physical and mental abuse, including bullying, can increase anxiety, as can current events such as increased work responsibility; insecurity within our faith, gender or relationships; money problems; or losing someone from our lives suddenly.

While these issues are all stressful, living in a constant state of anxiety means we can never fully experience the joys of being a human – we're always wondering, 'What if something bad happens?' That's why seeking support to manage an anxiety disorder has the potential to seriously improve our quality of life.

Types of anxiety

Because of our ability as humans to imagine the future and set goals and ambitions, it is easy for us to be restless or anxious about our current state. We're often seeking the next thing.

Anxiety and its terminology are quite nuanced. 'Anxiety' as a term is often interchangeable with 'stress', an emotion that can be felt by anyone. Feeling anxious about going on a date, running late for an appointment or doing an exam is normal, and the feeling will usually dissipate once the perceived threat (that our date won't like us, that we won't make our appointment time, or that we won't know the answers in the exam) passes. In fact, this feeling, while uncomfortable, is a surefire way to know we're alive! Known as *state anxiety*, this is when we become anxious because the things we value in life are threatened temporarily.

Some people are predisposed to being anxious because they tend to believe bad things are always going to happen or that the world is not a safe place. As this type of anxiety is baked into a person's personality, it is known as *trait anxiety*. Unlike state anxiety, trait anxiety is often genetically inherited and thus can be a little harder to manage. But it absolutely is possible!

Finally, *free-floating anxiety* is a type of anxiety that is sometimes caused by physiology, such as hormonal or biological changes. It's often hard to pinpoint the reason for anxious feelings when we're in this state, though increased caffeine intake, our menstrual cycles and hypervigilance can all cause free-floating anxiety.

When feelings of the above anxieties come about often and following minor stressors, they may actually be symptoms of an anxiety disorder. These feelings are more than just nerves – they are a form of mental illness that impacts our day-to-day activities, and prevents us from living healthily.

Anxiety disorders are diagnosed by a healthcare professional using the K10 tool, an evidence-based checklist that asks ten questions about feelings and emotions we've had over the previous four weeks. Questions aim to understand how tired we've been, how often we've been nervous, how often that nervousness has meant we could not calm down, how often we felt hopeless, and more.

Anxiety disorders are difficult to manage without help, and so people often seek therapy to understand techniques that can help to reduce or manage symptoms. In some cases, medication prescribed by a doctor or psychiatrist can also assist alongside talk therapy – and it is important to remember that taking prescribed medication should not be seen as a failure, but rather as a support to help you get your mind back to a good place.

There are six common anxiety disorders.

- **Post-traumatic stress disorder (PTSD)**: When a person who has experienced a traumatic event (often related to them or someone close to them being hurt) experiences nightmares, flashbacks, negative thoughts or intrusive images relating to the trauma.
- **Panic disorder**: When a person experiences panic attacks that are triggered with little reason or warning. Some symptoms of panic attacks include chest pain, shortness of breath, a feeling of choking, vertigo or a very overwhelming fear of death or doom.
- **Obsessive-compulsive disorder (OCD)**: When a person has consistent obsessions and unwanted distressing thoughts that are only relieved through compulsive and repetitive behaviours that disrupt their everyday routine. Prevalent obsessions for those with OCD can relate to cleanliness, symmetry, counting, hoarding, purity or harm (of themselves and others).

- **Specific phobias**: When a person has a specific, irrational fear related to a certain situation or thing, for example, going to the doctor, leaving the house, or spiders. Phobias can induce panic attacks, avoidance of the situation that causes fear, obsessive thoughts about the phobia and when it may next be encountered, and feelings of dread or terror when exposed to the phobia.
- **Social anxiety disorder**: When a person worries constantly about how others perceive them. More than harmless curiosity about the opinions of others, a person with social anxiety disorder has irrational fears of being judged, embarrassed or humiliated in public situations. People with social anxiety will often cancel plans or leave events early, tend not to be spontaneous, but on the flip side can especially dread events that are planned well in advance.
- **Generalised anxiety disorder (GAD)**: When a person is fearful and tense about a particular scenario without a reason, worrying excessively about one thing and then having their worries transfer to other scenarios without a clear connection.

Generalised anxiety disorder, also known as the 'worry disorder' for obvious reasons, is most common, impacting approximately 6 per cent of Australians in their lifetime, with 4 per cent of the population experiencing GAD in any twelve-month period.[2] This disorder makes living in the moment and enjoying life very difficult, with those of us diagnosed with generalised anxiety disorder tending to think 'What if?'. For instance:

- 'Everything is fine now, but what if something changes?'
- 'I love this person, but what if they don't love me?'
- 'I'm doing good work, but what if my boss doesn't think so?'

By constantly thinking in this negative pattern, which does not represent the facts as they are now, anxiety can get the better of us.

Common symptoms of GAD demonstrate the way the disorder affects our thoughts, bodily feelings and behaviour. It's important to note many of these symptoms are similar to those experienced during times of stress or worry. It is only when these symptoms are recurrent and long-lasting that they may be signs of GAD, diagnosable by a healthcare professional.

- **Thoughts:**
  - Focused attention on the thing we fear most
  - Limited ability to process new information
  - Inability to think clearly
  - 'I'm not good enough'
- **Bodily feelings:**
  - Triggered fight-or-flight response due to perceived threat
  - Increased heart rate and breathing
  - Tense muscles
  - Diarrhoea or tummy upset
  - Sleep difficulties
  - Panic attacks
- **Behaviour:**
  - Reduced productivity
  - Burnout
  - Poor performance and increased mistakes when doing a task
  - Forgetfulness
  - Agitation, demonstrated through fidgeting, nail biting or jumpiness
  - Increased substance use, such as drinking, smoking or eating poorly.

Fear about the future is a common trait of anxiety. Sometimes this can put us in a state of inactivity, where we freeze because it all feels too overwhelming. If we're in this state and not sure what to do next, we can try answering the following questions:

What would my kindest self do?	
What would my wisest self do?	
What would my bravest self do?	
What would my calmest self do?	
What would my truest self do?	
What would my happiest self do?	
What would my best self do?	

Exercise: Wise Mind

You can think of the mind as having three states: Reasonable, Emotional and Wise.[3] Your reasonable mind is driven by logic, your emotional mind is driven by feelings, and your wise mind is the balance between the two. Everyone possesses each of these states but most people gravitate towards a specific one most of the time. This exercise aims to give you the skill to find the wise mind when in moments of distress, and to respect your feelings while responding rationally.

When you're feeling anxious about a decision you need to make, take a deep breath and think about how you can activate your wise mind.

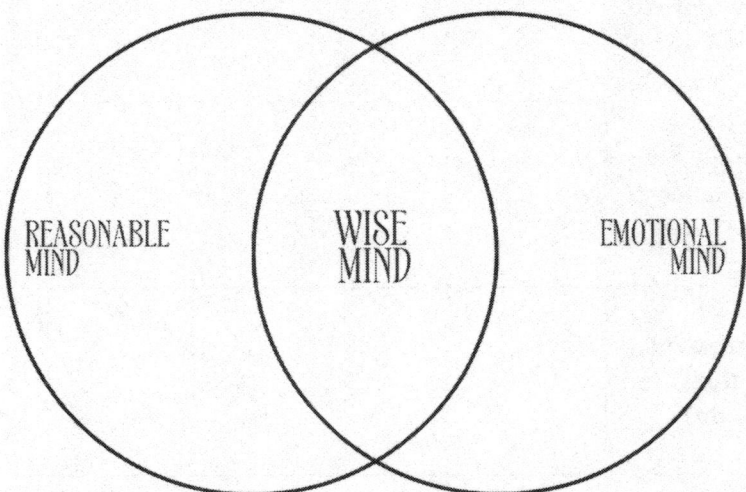

REASONABLE MIND

WISE MIND

EMOTIONAL MIND

- Focused and thoughtful.
- Slow to respond to situations.
- Task-oriented.
- Makes decisions based on facts.
- Approaches things objectively and intellectually.

- Lives mindfully.
- Values both intuition and wisdom.
- Balances reason and emotion.
- Respects feelings by recognising them, and responding to them rationally.

- Spontaneous.
- Quick to respond to situations.
- Likes intuition and hunches.
- Mood-dependent.
- Approaches things impulsively without considering the consequences.

Describe an experience you've had with each of the three states of mind:

EMOTIONAL: _____

_____

_____

e.g. cuddling a puppy you see on the street because it's adorable

REASONABLE: _____

_____

_____

e.g. not cuddling a puppy you see on the street because it may bite you

WISE: _____

_____

_____

e.g. asking the owner if you can cuddle their puppy and approaching it carefully

Anxiety as a discriminator

As we can tell from the above, anxiety is perceived as a threat to our sense of self, our identity. It's the fear we are not 'normal', and it feeds this fear by encouraging us to focus on the future instead of the present. Too often, we can miss out on the joy that is in the present due to worries about what's next. Unfortunately, due to many of the outside triggers discussed in chapter 2, more and more people are being diagnosed with anxiety disorders every day.

Anxiety and depressive disorders increased across the globe by 25 per cent during the pandemic.[4] However, there was also a slower decline in general life satisfaction taking place before the pandemic, especially in young people and groups such as the unemployed, those with fewer social connections, those in major cities and Indigenous peoples.[5]

According to the University of Melbourne's Household, Income and Labour Dynamics in Australia (HILDA) Survey, those aged between fifteen and thirty-four have reported sharp declines in mental health over the past decade.[6] While young people appear to have the worst mental health, there is some evidence that happiness increases as people age.[7]

Anxiety definitely discriminates along gender lines. More than a quarter of Australian women (27 per cent) are living with a diagnosed anxiety or depression disorder, compared to about 15 per cent of Australian men.[8] The reason for the disparity between genders is unknown, but is thought to include biological differences, such as brain chemistry and hormone fluctuation, as well as societal reasons – think the gender pay gap; the mental load carried by women, who are more often the primary carers of children and ageing parents, societal requirements to look and perform a certain way; and more. Social norms also impact men, who may feel pressure to hide their feelings for fear of being seen as 'weak'. This could also contribute to the lower figures for males – are they simply not seeking support, meaning that their mental health conditions are not captured? Transgender and gender-diverse Australians also face high rates of anxiety, reported to be a result of widespread discrimination, feelings of not belonging or barriers to employment.[9]

When I'm anxious, I get a tight chest, heart palpitations, hot or cold sweats. I shake uncontrollably, I stutter and lose my words. I get a red rash on my chest and I fidget. Sometimes, I burst into tears and less often I hyperventilate, collapse or even pass out as a result of my high-functioning anxiety, diagnosed after a car accident.

Fortunately, I manage my anxiety a lot better now than I did in the past. I take medication and I try to internalise my panic attacks unless they are just too big. Overthinking really doesn't help with anxiety, so I try to let things go, which is really quite challenging. I fill my days so that I don't have time to think too much, but then I have the challenge of trying not to burn myself out. The best I can do is try to dedicate more time out for myself and my own wellbeing.

Bek, 41
Gippsland, Victoria

Treating anxiety

If our anxious thoughts are getting into the way of our day-to-day activities, there are some strategies we can use to help us focus on the present and diminish anxious thoughts. Try the strategies listed below, and consider seeking support from a qualified professional who can help to keep you accountable, and share their own tools and tips for managing anxiety.

- **Do what scares you:** We may have a handful of activities that cause us regular anxiety. A nice way to challenge our anxious feelings is to commit to doing one thing that scares us each week. For instance, if you feel knots in your tummy when you give presentations at work, try volunteering to read publicly to your local library group first.
- **Journal out your worries:** The worry centre of the brain, the amygdala, can keep us up at night panicking. Switch it off by journalling about any fears you may have. Journalling doesn't need to be perfect or in the typical 'Dear Diary . . .' format – it just needs to be honest. Get a notebook you like and a pen with good flow, then sit down and write about your worries. Don't edit or pause to make it sound better than it needs to be. This is an exercise for you to simply acknowledge and purge the worries, leaving them on the page so you can get on with life.
- **Check your facts:** One of the best ways to manage anxiety is to assess the facts and bring ourselves back to the present. Anxiety

is a fear of the unknown, so a quick way to mitigate it is to try to stay in the present; in touch with what we know to be true. Ask yourself: 'What is true right now?', and 'How likely is it that what I'm worried about will happen?' Be honest with yourself; if you have anxious tendencies, you'll likely be catastrophising. Try the Decatastrophising exercise below to unpack catastrophic thoughts.

- **Forget perfectionism**: Perfectionist tendencies give a false sense of control, though they can also stop us from finishing a task. Choosing to move away from perfectionism helps us to accept the flaws and inconsistencies that are a part of life, and that make life the good kind of messy. Remember what Sheryl Sandberg, author and founder of women's equality organisation Lean In, says: 'Done is better than perfect.'[10]

- **Set time limits**: A practical way to behaviourally challenge our anxiety symptoms is to set time limits around the actions that feed them. For instance, if you worry about how your outfit will be perceived by others at university or work, you may choose to give yourself only twenty minutes to get ready and out the door – removing the opportunity to think and rethink through your outfit choice. Or, if you're so concerned with tidiness that you're vacuuming three times per week, you might schedule five days of after-work activities so that the time allowance for vacuuming is reduced to only two days per week.

- **Get real about who cares**: Always making yourself smaller because you're worried what other people think of you? No one cares as much about us as we think they do. In fact, they may even be worried about what *we* think of *them*.

- **Practise relaxation**: If someone tells us to 'Just relax!' when we're in a state of anxiety, we can almost guarantee it won't help! However, having a handful of relaxation techniques up our own sleeves for those moments can be handy. Relaxation can slow down our heart rate, reduce blood pressure and muscle tension, and slow our breathing – counteracting the symptoms of anxiety. Try mindfulness, deep breathing (see the Box Breathing exercise on page 196) and meditation, or discover a unique activity that relaxes you, such as drawing, walking in the bush or playing with your cat.

- **Prepare coping statements**: Coping statements are short facts or challenges that we can have close at hand to help us push an anxious thought away. These can range from 'This too shall pass' to 'Will this matter in twenty-four hours?' to 'Not a disaster, just a small inconvenience'. Whichever coping statement best works for you, the trick is to have it readily visible as a constant reminder. For instance, a Post-it note that reads 'I have the right to be here' placed somewhere you can see it on your wheelchair may help you push anxious thoughts away when you go to a festival with friends.
- **Share your mental load**: Sometimes, simply talking about our worries can help halve them. Identify someone you can share your mental load with. This may be a trusted friend, a partner or your parents. Any good friend should be non-judgemental and open to listening to your concerns about life. However, if you can't find someone to speak with regularly, consider a therapist or journalling to get worrying thoughts out of your head.

Exercise: Decatastrophising

Commonly called 'spiralling', 'ruminating' or a 'negative spiral', catastrophising is the act of getting so worked up in your mind that you believe the worst possible outcome to be likely or even unavoidable. Catastrophising thoughts often exaggerate problems beyond reality, and they can harm us if the pattern continues to occur.

Decatastrophising is the act of challenging catastrophic thoughts to bring your feelings back to facts and reality, putting a stop to distorted thinking. This exercise is similar to Socratic Questioning (see page 115), though is best used when worries are extreme or worst-case.

Here is an example of using Decatastrophising on a catastrophic thought spiral concerning failing an upcoming test.

What am I worried about?	*If I don't pass this test, then I will fail the course, which means I won't be able to get a promotion, which means I can't support my family, which means I will end up on the streets, which means my friends won't want to be my friends anymore, which means . . .*
Is this worry likely to come true? What evidence is there to support this?	*Maybe. I didn't pass the last test, but I also didn't study for that one. I have been studying for this test.*
Okay, if this worry does come true, what's the *worst* thing that could happen?	*I fail the test, which means I fail the course . . . But I do have the option to try it again in six months' time. This would delay the course completion by only six months.*
But if this worry doesn't come true, what's the *more likely* thing to happen?	*I pass this test. I'm nervous, so I may not get a great score, but I have been studying so I'll know I've done my best.*
Imagine this worry comes true. How will I feel in one week from now?	*So upset. It's going to make me feel ashamed and like I'm not good enough.*
What about one month from now?	*I would have gotten over it a bit better, and I could be focusing on taking the test again in six months' time.*
And how would I feel one year from now?	*It won't matter if I manage to pass the second test. If I had failed the first one, I would have applied myself extra hard for the one in six months. I should be okay in one year!*

In the above example, the person comes to understand that it's not the end of the world if they don't get a good grade in this one test.

Use the Decatastrophising template opposite on an unhelpful thought spiral you often have.

What am I worried about?	
Is this worry likely to come true? What evidence is there to support this?	
Okay, if this worry does come true, what's the *worst* thing that could happen?	
But if this worry doesn't come true, what's the *more likely* thing to happen?	
Imagine this worry comes true. How will I feel in one week from now?	
What about one month from now?	
And how would I feel one year from now?	

Exercise: Box Breathing

Beloved by Navy Seals, the Box Breathing technique – also known as four-square breathing – is a simple 'do anywhere' exercise that can help you stay calm and improve concentration in tense situations. By completing this technique, and breathing at a considerably slower speed, your heart rate will slow way down and any feelings of anxiety or overwhelm can be reduced.

If possible, sit up in a chair with your feet on the floor. Then close your eyes and relax your posture.

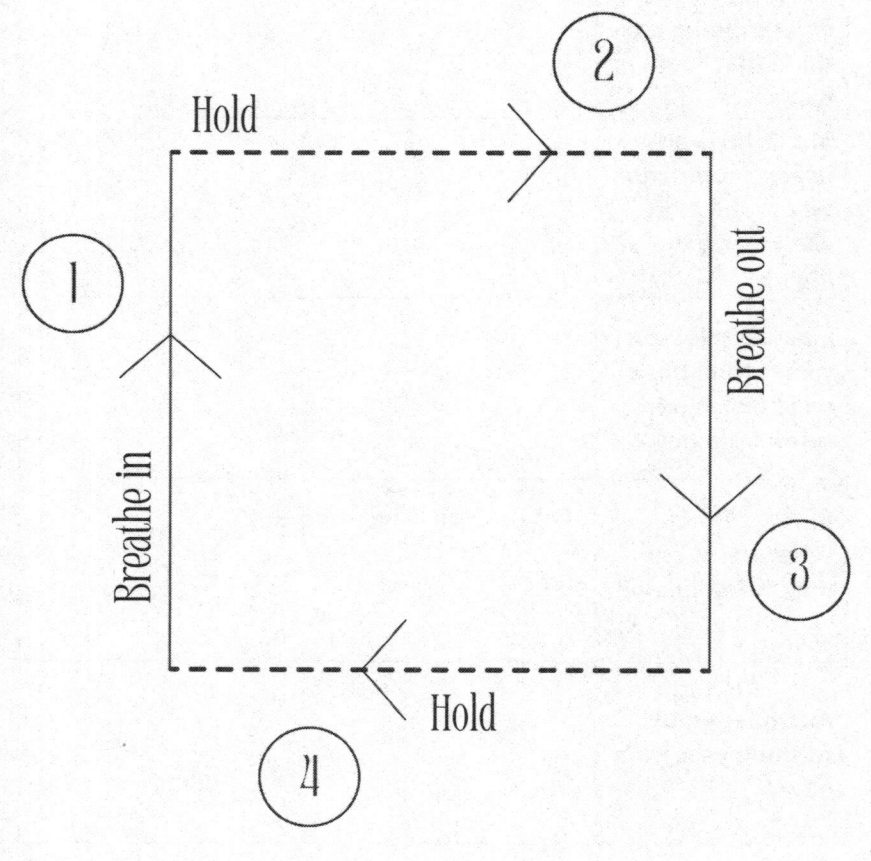

1. Breathe in through the nose while counting to four. Do this slowly, and take notice of the air entering into your lungs.
2. Hold your breath now, counting to four, with a 'soft' mouth and nose (don't clamp them shut).
3. Breathe out through your mouth while counting to four. Again, do this slowly and take notice of the air exiting your lungs.
4. Hold your breath once more, counting to four and with your 'soft' mouth and nose.

Now repeat the steps above, up to five times or for as long as you need.

During your in and out breaths, try to completely fill and empty your lungs. Breathe in deeply for the full four seconds until you absolutely cannot fit any more air in your lungs. When breathing out, exhale slowly so that almost no air remains in your lungs.

The most important takeaway from this chapter is that anxiety does not define us. You can be a *person troubled by anxiety*; you are not an *anxious person*. Thinking of it this way externalises the disorder and separates it from ourselves, making these feelings easier to manage.

Using an anxiety disorder to describe or define ourselves can actually make things worse. By focusing attention on our anxieties, we can give them more space in our lives than they deserve. Don't fuel the fire.

When things feel overwhelming, take three deep breaths – focusing on inhaling and exhaling deeply can do wonders for our mental health in anxious moments. Whether we're experiencing everyday stress and worry, or have been diagnosed with a more serious anxiety disorder, the tips and techniques within this chapter can help us to manage our symptoms. But if you ever feel that your anxiety is out of your control and having a serious impact on your health and wellbeing, it's important to seek professional help (see chapter 17 for more information).

Chapter 14

Down, but not out

Coping with sadness, grief and depression

Every single one of us has experienced sadness. From losing our favourite toy when we are little, to missing our primary school friends when we go off to high school, to experiencing our first gut-wrenching heartbreak or the death of someone we love. Sadness can feel all-consuming, like we'll never get past the feelings of numbness, weight, or loss. Until one day, somehow, we do.

Often, we become sad because of something we experience, and when we resolve these experiences, the behaviours that come with sadness – crying, self-isolating, eating unhealthily or skipping meals – also dissipate. The beauty of these behaviours, though, is in their catharsis. It can feel incredibly soothing to cry, which is why we tend to gravitate towards television shows with deeply emotional plot lines (hello, *Grey's Anatomy*) or albums that have us scream-crying on the way home from work (and hello, Adele).

Sadness is a very common emotion, and our levels of resilience against feeling sad differ from day to day. For instance, you may feel incredibly strong one week, and then see an older couple kissing on the street and burst into tears. Many factors could have triggered you to feel sad at this moment – perhaps you've just ended a relationship, or lost a grandparent, or are about to start menstruating, or haven't seen your mum in months, or perhaps the older work colleague you were close to has just retired to be with their ailing wife.

Our level of resilience when dealing with sadness also differs from person to person. Typically, it is not an emotion that interferes with our day-to-day functioning – we may feel sad for only a few minutes before the feeling passes. More severe moments of sadness, though, could be a symptom of something else.

Grief

While the terms 'grief', 'sadness' and 'depression' are often used inter-changeably, they are not the same. Think of sadness as a symptom of grief, which itself is an appropriate response to loss. Meanwhile, depression is the result of brain chemistry imbalance (see page 203 for more on this).

Grief is the emotional manifestation of losing something or some-one. This may be a parent, a friend or a pet, or it may be something less tangible – such as the future we were looking forward to with our partner that has now changed following the relationship breakdown, or our self-identity following the loss of a job or a life-changing medical diagnosis.

People experience grief in many ways and at different depths; however, there are some similarities that most of us can relate to. These include:

- Depressive symptoms, such as feeling low, numb, in denial, empty or lonely
- Anger, guilt, blame and relief if the relationship with the person/thing that is lost was complicated
- Loss of appetite, headaches, difficulty sleeping, a weakened immune system, dull chest pain (hence the term 'broken heart')
- Constant and overwhelming sadness that eventually dissipates into waves that may recur when we're triggered by certain memories – no matter how small.

There are ways to honour the people, pets and even the futures that we have lost, in a way that reduces the impact on our daily lives over time. Healthy grieving is an active process – something we need to choose to do – and there are steps we can take to make it easier:

- **Taking our time**: Grief does not happen on a timeline. Our feelings are valid, and we should feel them in a way that makes us comfortable – with loved ones, by ourselves or with a therapist.
- **Crying it out**: Crying is not weak. It is a healthy, cathartic release of overwhelming emotions. When we look at it like that, crying can help us to feel better sooner. Let it out.
- **Seeking support**: While grieving in our own way is important, we can find solace with those who are also grieving or have experienced a similar grief previously. Talking about how we feel and how those around us who experienced grief got through it can help share the load.
- **Honouring and accepting the loss**: Don't try to push thoughts of the person, pet or thing that you're grieving out of your mind. Instead, we can honour their memory by keeping a picture or memento of them close by, raising a glass to them at group celebrations, or talking about their great qualities with loved ones. This can help us accept the finality of the loss while keeping their memory alive – an important step in finding closure.
- **Rewriting the future**: If it's a certain style of future we're grieving, it's important to take the time to acknowledge what that may have looked like before making new plans. Without going too far in advance, we can then focus on what we would like our new future to look like now it has been shaped by loss. For example, maybe we won't be going to Europe with our partner next year anymore, but perhaps we could put the money we saved into something just for ourselves – like a road trip down the coast with our best friend.
- **Knowing that we can grow around grief**: Though loss can seem overwhelming, with time we learn to grow around our grief. This doesn't mean we've stopped caring, only that we've become better able to bear the burden. Knowing this can help us manage any feelings of guilt that surrounds the grief.

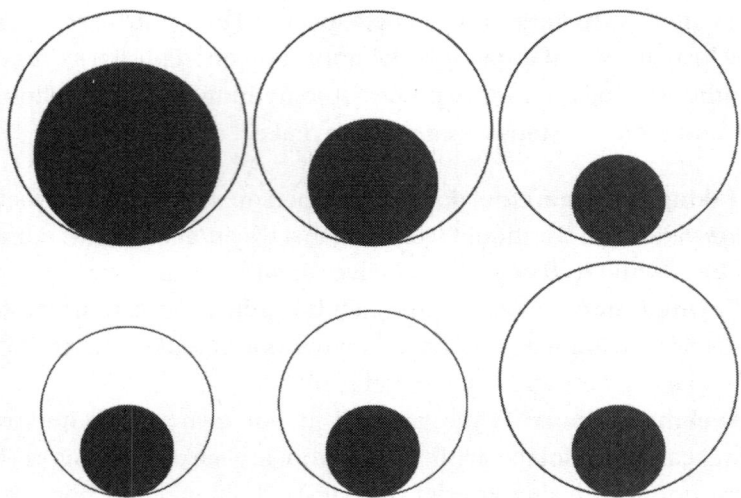

Figure 14.1 A person's grief does not shrink as time passes (top). Instead, we learn to grow our lives around the grief each day (bottom).

Importantly, remember that showing signs of grief is not a weakness. It is a strength and a coping mechanism. Please do seek support from a therapist to assist with grief management if you feel this could help. Because after all, what is grief if not love persevering?[1]

When grieving, your whole world shrinks to a pinpoint. Nothing else registers or matters. The only thing you can focus on is what has happened and how it feels. I'm lucky enough to have an amazing partner and after our first miscarriage we just held each other and cried and talked – about everything we were thinking and feeling. Small things and big things. Hard things and funny things.

Eventually the colour seeps back into things that faded away. Your world slowly brightens and you get through. The hurt is always there but not quite so vivid and all-consuming.

Getting through builds resilience and strength and self-belief. When we miscarried again, and again, I knew we would get through. But the knowledge was purely intellectual. It didn't help me move through the grief any faster. I knew I would get there, but I still had dark days and a lot of sadness and anger.

For me, talking about things always helps, whether that's with my partner, family, friends or a counsellor. It's not about finding a solution, but about naming and acknowledging what's going on.

Matilda, 42
Hunter Valley, New South Wales

Depression

One of the main differences between sadness and depression is how long this emotional state sticks around. Sadness is more transient, coming and going when things happen in our lives to make us feel down. With sadness, we're usually able to work through it in time and with support, going back to normal activities within weeks, sometimes days. Depression – a mood disorder – persists long past its welcome and can be so extreme that it impacts our ability to think and act clearly or hold onto positive relationships. Symptoms usually ebb and flow, though they can slowly cause us to sink deeper into a poor mood when they stick around.

Depression is one of the two most common mood disorders, alongside bipolar disorder. It's also Australia's second most prevalent mental health condition, behind anxiety.[2] There's a saying sometimes attributed to Chinese philosopher Lao Tzu: 'If you are depressed you are living in the past. If you are anxious you are living in the future. If you are at peace you are living in the present.'

As we get older, it's easy to long for previous joys we had in life. We may no longer feel as attractive, as popular, as successful or as happy as we used to be. All of us experience loss in life – loss of a person, a thing, a physical ability, mental clarity, our youth . . . these can result in sadness, grief, anxiety, anger and more. But when melancholy turns to hopelessness that is hard to shake over time – even when we're smiling on the outside – we may be experiencing a depressive disorder.

> *I had feelings of emptiness and worthlessness, intrusive or suicidal thoughts, self-harm, dissociation, poor hygiene, over-eating or undereating, low motivation or even no motivation. I also drank, isolated myself socially and had anxiety.*
>
> **Ashira, 26**
> **Melbourne, Victoria**

Diagnosable by a therapist using the K10 tool, major depression can manifest with a variety of negative symptoms, both psychological and physical. While society may sometimes portray it as such, depression doesn't always take the form of crying and suicidal ideation. Symptoms persist for an extended period, and can include any of the below:

- Very low energy
- Overeating or not eating at all
- Changes in sleep habits, such as difficulty sleeping or sleeping too much
- Recurrent thoughts of suicide or self-harm
- Faking a smile or not smiling with your eyes
- Distancing yourself emotionally from other people
- Feelings of guilt, worthlessness, sadness, loneliness or irritability
- Loss of motivation and interest in activities you used to previously enjoy
- Calling in sick, often, to work or school
- The feeling of being stuck in a fog, weighed down by something all-consuming, feeling 'flat' or 'numb'
- Isolating from friends, family and avoiding social events
- Self-harming to find relief or distract yourself, through cutting, punching, burning or sticking sharp objects into your skin
- Forgoing basic hygiene habits such as showering, brushing your hair or changing your clothing.

Types of depression

While major depression described above is the more common depressive disorder experienced in Australia, there are other acute types of depression that share similar symptoms, including:

- **Seasonal affective disorder (SAD)**: Do you find yourself in a sad mood when the weather is overcast or rainy, especially over several days? Seasonal affective disorder, suitably known as SAD, is a very real depressive disorder that we most often experience in winter. Luckily, the winters in Australia aren't as bad as in other countries, where days are much shorter and the exposure to natural light is limited. As such, we generally experience SAD for a few months at most.
- **Melancholic depression**: Those who experience severe melancholic depression describe feeling 'numb' to everything. They find it difficult to sleep, feel sluggish and cannot react to or find much pleasure in life, even when something positive happens.
- **Postnatal depression (PND)**: Experienced by one in seven Australian women who have just given birth,[3] postnatal depression tends to last more than two weeks and can interfere with caring for a new baby. Symptoms include those experienced with major depression as well as irrational fears for a baby's or partner's safety. Around 40 per cent of women who experience PND find it begins during pregnancy.
- **Psychotic major depression**: This occurs when symptoms of major depression are accompanied by hallucinations and delusions.
- **Atypical depression**: If a person experiences many symptoms of major depression but not enough to be officially diagnosed, they could have atypical depression. Most commonly, symptoms are weight gain due to an increase in appetite, sensitivity to rejection and difficulty getting out of bed.

Major depression is most often caused by either a trigger, such as a stressful life circumstance (this is known as reactive or situational depression), or by biology, where there is an imbalance in the brain's biochemicals (this is known as chemical depression). Common biological causes of depression include illness from the overuse of and withdrawal from illicit substances, neurological disorders such as multiple sclerosis or epilepsy, endocrine disorders such as diabetes, and fluctuations of sex hormones. For instance, people who menstruate may experience premenstrual dysphoric disorder (PMDD). More serious than premenstrual syndrome (PMS) – whose common tropes include craving chocolate or getting angrier ahead of menstruating – PMDD adds feelings of serious depression to the mix for anything from a few days to several weeks ahead of menstruation.

The inability of our brain to regulate certain neurotransmitters, such as serotonin, can be both a cause *and* a symptom of depression, and though depressive disorders can sometimes run in families, there is not always a genetic predisposition involved. Regardless of what causes it, depression can make us wonder 'Why me?', which in turn can send us into a deeper feeling of hopelessness. This is why it's important to treat our depressive symptoms as soon as we're able.

I want to tell people with depressive symptoms to not give up. Don't give up on yourself, the system and your future. You deserve the life you have been given, and it won't always be or feel like this. You are so much more capable than you think. Don't be afraid to reach out for help and support because you are not alone, not a burden, and people do want to see you thrive.

Ashira, 26
Melbourne, Victoria

Managing depression

The number one thing to remember when it comes to depression is that you are not alone. It's a common disorder among Australians, but it does not define us. We can challenge the thoughts, feelings and behaviours we succumb to when in a depressive episode by:

- **Identifying protective factors**: Who are the people we can go to if we need support? What are the things that make life worth living? Who depends on us to be here, on this Earth, such as a pet, a child, a parent? These are all our protective factors, our reasons for living. Identify and think of them when times get tough.
- **Using positive language**: The different ways we think and speak about depression can add to the weight of it, or help us deal with its symptoms. For example, which of these statements makes depression seem more manageable: 'You are currently experiencing a depressive disorder' or 'You are depressed'? The former makes it easier to work on managing the disorder (something we *are experiencing*), rather than feeling that it is actually an intrinsic part of us (something we *are*), as the latter implies. Language is important. Focus on the solution instead of the problem: what we can do about the state we're in.
- **Telling others that we're suffering**: Our family and friends will want to know if we're hurting. How much we actually tell them is a personal decision, but sometimes a simple 'I'm having a rough day' is enough to flag to them that we need to be nurtured. This can be especially difficult in the workplace. If you're comfortable, it can be helpful to identify a colleague (ideally one you report to) and tell them about your diagnosis. You can explain to them that you know it's unusual to speak to them about your mental health, but that you want them to know – so that when you say you're having a bad day and need to plug in the headphones to distract yourself from external triggers like loud colleagues, they'll allow it. Of course, every workplace is different – try to find a close support that works for you.
- **Taking medication**: There's still a bit of stigma around taking medication for our mental health, but there absolutely shouldn't be. Why wouldn't we take something that makes us feel better?

Prescribed medications can do wonders for managing depression, but many come with side effects. That's why it's important to monitor your mood closely and report back to your doctor, who should arrange regular check-ins. The most common medications for depression in Australia are selective serotonin reuptake inhibitors (SSRIs), also commonly used to treat anxiety. These take time to work on your body, sometimes as long as four weeks, so it's best to stick with them and manage any side effects with the help of your doctor. And remember, when the medication starts to work and you feel better, it doesn't mean you should stop taking it without speaking to your doctor first. You feel better because it's working!

Supplements such as vitamin B12, fish oil and zinc can also help our mood. Ask your doctor for a blood test to check your vitamin levels, and always check with them before starting any complementary medicines.

- **Challenging depressive thinking**: As with anxiety, it's important to challenge negative thoughts and separate fiction from fact if we have depression. In the case of depression, we can try to shift our negative thoughts ('I am worthless and don't contribute anything to society') to rational ones ('I am worthy, and I do contribute by making my friends laugh/producing good art/helping my company meet its targets').

- **Building self-esteem**: Depression is linked with poor self-esteem. We can build our self-esteem by reminding ourselves what we're good at, living by our values, looking after our basic hygiene, trying new looks with our clothes or hair, and doing things we enjoy.

- **Moving and eating well**: Our diet is a huge part of our mental health. Some studies have shown that diets high in fresh whole foods and water decrease the risk of depression, while processed meats and foods high in fat and refined sugars increase the risk.[4] In addition, moving our body for just thirty minutes per day has been shown to help alleviate depressive symptoms.[5]

Research has consistently found a clear association between the quality of one's diet and their risk of developing depression, with a significant number of studies proving the role of good nutrition to treat mental illness. Improving your gut health can help to improve mental health, and conversely, negative changes to your gut health can negatively impact mood. Gut microbes produce and respond to neurohormones like serotonin, dopamine, and others. With intestinal serotonin able to influence mood, appetite, sleep, and brain function, it's important to eat the right foods.

I recommend following a Mediterranean-style diet, with a key focus on foods that provide: omega-3 fatty acids, such as walnuts, fish, flax seeds, chia seeds, hemp seeds and leafy greens; phytochemicals, such as herbs, spices, fruit, vegetables, wholegrains, nuts, seeds, coffee, black tea, green tea and red wine; B vitamins, such as from leafy greens, wholegrains, fish, meat and eggs; vitamin D, via sunlight or a supplement in winter months; anthocyanins and glucosinolates, found in blueberries and broccoli respectively, both nutrients that help your brain work better; and bioactive compounds that can improve your mental health, such as those found in extra virgin olive oil.

Chloe McLeod, accredited practising dietitian

- **Scheduling positive activities**: What are the simple, little things you enjoy most in life? Whether it's the first coffee of the day, moving up a level in our favourite video game or making little clay pots with our own bare hands, scheduling the things that bring us joy can make our days feel happier. Use the Five Joyful Things exercise below to remind yourself what makes your heart sing.
- **Setting goals**: Crossing something off our to-do list or achieving a small goal gives us a tiny rush of dopamine, the reward chemical. Set – and write down – small goals like 'walk around the block', 'cook myself a nutritious dinner' or 're-read my favourite book'. Each time you cross an achievement off your list, you'll get a natural high!

- **Pursuing passions**: Discovering what drives us can give our life purpose and make it worth living. But it's important to remember our purpose doesn't have to be a huge thing like 'stop climate change' (although we should all do our part). Instead, it can be something small that we can hold onto. For instance, maybe you love animals. This doesn't mean you need to head off on the Sea Shepherd for months at a time. Instead, why not consider fostering a puppy who needs a home from your local rescue centre? By focusing your attention on your new passion – this puppy – you will be distracted from spiralling sad thoughts as you instead focus on loving and caring for Fido. Plus, it will force you to get outside for a walk for exercise and won't let you stay in bed all day – someone needs to take the puppy outside to pee!

- **Seeking social support, even though it's the last thing we feel like doing**: Yes, we'll want to isolate ourselves from others when we're down. But try not to. For example, we can arrange a social outing with a close mate. This doesn't need to be a big deal where we get dressed up or leave our own neighbourhood to see them. Instead, we could throw on some sweats and a cap and go for a walk around the park. Our friends won't care what we look like, just that we're willing to chat to them. Saying how we feel will never ruin a real connection.

———

Fighting depression is hard, and we will have days when it feels insurmountable. We will withdraw from others and fuel our depression by sitting in the dark, avoiding calls, reading negative articles or blogs online, and worrying about something we did days, months or years in the past. It's important not to stay in this space, but to accept our situation and choose to move on as best we can. This can feel impossible to do on our own, though, so we shouldn't go it alone. Seek support from a close friend, family member, teacher, colleague or therapist you trust. If you can't think of anyone or you don't want to bother them (a real, but unfounded thought process), call or text a mental health service (see page 245 for a list of organisations), or visit your GP and ask for a Mental Health Treatment Plan.

Exercise: Five Joyful Things

By practising the simple act of gratitude and reminding ourselves that life is not all bad, the Five Joyful Things exercise helps you to remember the wonderful things in life when you're feeling low.

On the next page, write down five things that bring you joy. These should be easily attainable and not dependent on anything external, such as another person or loads of money. Some examples include 'a really good cup of coffee', 'putting my bare feet in the grass', 'feeling the sun on my face', 'my dog running to greet me when I get home'.

Once you've written your Five Joyful Things below, take a photo of the page or copy them out onto a Post-it note that you can stick on your bathroom mirror or work desk. Your list should always be close by, so you can access it when you feel down, and you should try to take a conscious step towards doing at least one of your Five Joyful Things every single day.

If you feel comfortable, share your Five Joyful Things with me on social media. Perhaps we can all get inspiration from one another's lists: #PaperbackTherapy.

My Five Joyful Things are...

1.

2.

3.

4.

5.

When my friend Michele died, many people asked, 'How could someone like her have been so depressed?' She was driven, inspiring, doing well in her career, happy in her relationship, confident, kind and so beautiful. It really highlighted how little we all know about, or perhaps pay attention to, depression.

Loving Michele through depression made me feel so many things – helpless, frustrated, inspired, hopeful, heartbroken, disconnected. It taught me so much, too. While I wish with everything I have that I could have saved my friend, I hope that the lessons I've learned can be shared with others and together, we can do better.

Depression is a societal issue. We need to stop putting all of the onus on the individual and start to change our behaviour too. We need to support and assist those struggling just as we would someone with a disability. Of course, there are lots of nuances and the person has to want to be helped, but I have learned that change starts with all of us. When we know better, we do better and I will never stop trying.

Kelly, 39
Northern Rivers, New South Wales

Suicide

For some people, suicide may feel like the only 'way out' of depression. But this isn't the case: there are people who want to, and can, help. It is estimated that more than 10 million Australian adults know someone who has died by suicide, and may have had no idea that their friend or family member was suffering with depression or planning to end their life.[6] There are, though, common risk factors, including:

- **Gender**: Despite women attempting suicide more often than men, it is men who are at higher risk of dying by suicide. In fact, Australian men accounted for 75 per cent of deaths by suicide in the 2021 census.[7]

- **First Nations background**: Indigenous Australians are twice as likely to die by suicide than non-Indigenous Australians.[8]
- **Age**: Risk of suicide increases in middle age, with the highest proportion of deaths by suicide occurring between 30 and 59 years old.[9] In addition, 34 per cent of deaths among 15–17-year-olds in 2021 were due to suicide. That proportion was 35 per cent for Australians aged 18–24 years.[10]
- **Frequent thoughts of suicide**: While it's no guarantee, a person who thinks about suicide often is likely to have increased risk of following through on those thoughts.
- **Established plans**: If a person has moved from thinking about suicide in the vague sense to establishing a plan, their risk is increased.
- **Method availability**: If a person has the means to follow through with their plan, such as having access to a weapon, their risk is increased.
- **Relationship, financial or medical problems**: Personal problems such as those with a spouse, best friend or parent; financial problems; or medical problems (e.g. a disability or terminal diagnosis) can increase a person's risk of suicide.
- **Suicide completion by a friend or family member**: Risk of suicide is increased when a person has lost someone close to them by suicide.
- **Loss**: The death of a loved one, job, home, pet or something else of great value can contribute to a person's suicide risk.
- **Loneliness**: A lack of protective factors – such as connections within a person's community, workplace, family and friendship groups – can decrease the will to stay connected to the world.
- **Substance use and risky behaviour**: Accomplished suicide is associated with increased use of drugs and alcohol, possibly because substance use reduces inhibitions. In addition, a person who participates in risky behaviour, such as being especially (and unsafely) promiscuous or driving recklessly, may be more at risk.
- **Trauma**: Traumatic events such as abuse, bullying and neglect – whether emotional, physical, social or sexual – can contribute to suicide risk.

- **Giving away possessions:** Ending a contract, giving prized possessions away to other people or updating a will can all be characteristics
of a person planning suicide, especially when combined with other
indications.

While people may experience suicidal thoughts when living with
depression, this doesn't always lead to suicide. Lack of motivation as a
symptom of depression can often act as a preventative measure, foiling
the preparation required for someone to make and follow through with
a suicide plan. It is important that, regardless of your own thoughts
about whether a person will move ahead with it, any talk of suicide is
taken seriously. Intervention by a professional such as a doctor, therapist or person of authority should be sought immediately.

*Sometimes I feel like I have no feelings, I can't feel anything.
That's when I know I'm having a bit of a flare-up of depression.
If I receive an accolade or something amazing happens, I feel I
have nothing inside of me to allow me to enjoy that experience.
I get sad and teary and feel completely alone. I don't reach out
or talk to anyone about it, and simply wait for it to pass. It feels
heavy and like there's no end in sight. I am learning to just be
kind to myself, as much as I can – to ask myself, 'What do I need
right now that is good for me?' and give myself that thing.*

Bek, 41
Gippsland, Victoria

A therapist can help you manage depressive and suicidal thoughts
by removing the shame associated with both topics and bringing them
into the room. They can help you discuss why you may feel hopeless
at this moment, through direct questioning about the root cause and
frequency of your feelings. If you're unable to seek therapy, you can try
the following exercise to identify your protective factors and support
systems, which can help to remind you that you are not alone and that
you have a reason to stay on this Earth.

MY PROTECTIVE FACTORS Who am I here for?	MY SUPPORT SYSTEM Who is here for me?
e.g. My cat, Mao, who I feed and give pats to	e.g. My work wife, Emily
e.g. My devil's ivy plant, which I need to water weekly	e.g. My partner, Alain

There are many ways to fight feelings of sadness, grief and depression. But we are most likely to be successful in our battle if we reach out to our support network, take proactive steps to manage our symptoms, and remind ourselves of all the things in life that bring us joy and make us feel grateful. If you are experiencing severe depression or suicidal thoughts, it is important to seek immediate help by phoning your GP or a support service such as Lifeline (13 11 14). See page 245 for a full list of crisis support numbers.

Part Three

Help is at Hand

Chapter 15

Lean on me

How to help a loved one in crisis

Sometimes it's not us who is struggling with mental health, but someone very close to us. It can be incredibly hard to see our friends or family members struggle and, understandably, we may not know what to say or do.

Here is a non-exhaustive list of signs that a loved one may be struggling with their mental health:

- **They are neglecting their personal hygiene**: They are no longer brushing their hair, dressing as they used to, bothering to shower, etc.
- **They become withdrawn**: They are no longer reaching out to chat or to meet up, or they are cancelling plans more often than is usual. We may notice changes in texting patterns: a friend who was previously quick to respond is now replying infrequently.
- **Their eyes have lost their 'sparkle'**: They just aren't their usual happy self. We can feel something is wrong, deep in our gut.
- **They have difficulty doing 'everyday' tasks**: They tell us they have been unable to sleep or are sleeping too much, or that they can no longer concentrate at work or at school.

- **They have little regard for life**: They participate in riskier behaviour than usual, such as skipping work or school, drinking or taking drugs, driving erratically, etc.
- **Their body has changed drastically**: We notice significant weight loss or gain, or marks on their skin that cannot be explained.
- **They tell us in a roundabout way**: They want to discuss feeling hopeless, angry or sad, or they talk about death, but are tearful or distant when doing so; they are worrying about things that did not previously bother them or that are unlikely to happen.

One of the things therapists look for when doing a case presentation is what their client's protective factors are. These are the things in our lives that promote good mental health through connection, such as physical health and healthy behaviours, strong cultural identity and community inclusion, people who depend on us (children, elderly parents or pets) and our social support system (our friends, family, community and colleagues). And when a loved one is suffering, we can be a valuable part of their social support system, which is one of the best protective factors a person can have.

A social support is a person we feel we can go to when everything goes sideways. They're someone who will listen to us without judgement, who will hug us when we don't even think we need a hug, and who will keep our feelings protected because that's what's important to us. The glitch is, though, that often it's hard to recognise our social support when we're in a moment of crisis.

When you notice that a loved one is struggling, it's important to check in proactively. The most important thing we can do is simply remind them that we are there for them and that we love them. Remember, even if you're not sure what to say, the act of listening can help. A simple reply of, 'I don't know what to say, but I'm here for you' goes a long way.

Tips for helping a loved one in crisis

Here are some other ways we can help someone we care about who we believe is in crisis.

Be a buddy

A 'mental health buddy' is a person we can count on to reach out to when we're experiencing a bad day. By officially designating ourselves as a loved one's mental health buddy, we are telling them that they can contact us any time for a chat, and vice versa.

Decide how you would best like to be reached and establish this with your loved one. Create a 'mental health buddy' WhatsApp group or Instagram DM as a reminder that you're there for one another.

Start a conversation

Talking about our feelings can be hard, especially if we're not used to doing so. Choosing a moment when our loved one is relaxed will encourage them to open up. Supporting them means learning about their trauma and their triggers, and ensuring we work around these as best we can during discussions – within our capacity to do so. A successful conversation will not see us sacrifice our needs, safety or wellbeing to help someone else.

The language we use when supporting someone in need is important. Asking open questions that encourage our loved one to answer in sentences rather than with 'yes' or 'no' will help us to understand where their feelings are stemming from, and to identify any risks of self-harm. A nice way to do this is to check in ('How are you feeling today?') rather than check up ('Do you still feel sad today?').

Brené Brown writes about the difference between empathy (feeling *with* people) and sympathy (feeling *for* people) in *Dare to Lead*. Empathy drives connection whereas sympathy fosters disconnection. Don't worry about being perfect or saying the wrong thing, it's better to start a conversation than not at all.

Your friend may not open up to you right away, but they will know that you are there for them when they next feel ready to talk. Don't underestimate how big that is.

Don't keep it a secret

It's likely our loved one will want us to keep the conversations we have with them private, but if these stray into the topic of self-harm or abuse, we should definitely tell someone we trust. While they may be upset at first if they find out we've broken their trust, we may potentially be saving their life.

Help them access happiness

It is possible to 'switch on' happiness chemicals by performing simple tasks.

The neurotransmitter dopamine is a chemical released in our nervous system that helps us to feel pleasure and reward. Listening to music or doing something creative with a loved one who is suffering can release dopamine, as can encouraging them to seek new experiences or accomplish small tasks, like finishing a book or a puzzle.

Another neurotransmitter is serotonin, a happiness and wellbeing chemical that we can access through exercise, meditation, eating healthy foods and even basking in the sunshine. Consider taking your loved one for a yummy salad picnic in the park and going for an easy walk afterwards – it could put them in a better mood.

Share resources with them

We often share interests with our friends, and we can dive deep into those as a means to reach out when a loved one is self-isolating due to mental health. Share articles or memes that you come across that you know they'll love, or a link to a (happy!) podcast about a topic you've discussed in the past.

Simple tasks can seem daunting when we are in crisis. Send your loved one a gift box of items to use in the shower or a ready-cook meal kit so that the task of washing or eating, which may feel insurmountable to them, is made easier.

You can also share the insights you have gained from reading *Paperback Therapy* with your loved one, or direct them to the @bare_therapy Instagram page for access to therapist-approved insights and tools, straight to their phone.

Remind them of the good

When we are spiralling and feeling severely depressed, it can be very difficult for us to find the good in life. Everything seems boring or worthless, and things we used to like will go unnoticed.

Reminding our loved one of the good things in life can positively impact their mental health by separating facts ('Some things are bad') from fiction ('Everything is the worst'). We can help by sharing with them the good things that are happening right now, such as by taking them to a dog park to see puppies running around, going to their place to watch a film we loved as kids, or texting them when it's a full moon and telling them to get outside and see it. By reminding them to focus on the good in the present instead of dwelling on or reminiscing about the past, we're demonstrating to them that there are things worth living for and enjoying, here and now.

Refer them to professional support

One of the easiest and best things we can do for a loved one who is struggling is share with them the details of a professional therapist or support person (doctor, youth worker, or teacher) we feel may help them. Use the tips in the 'Seeking professional help' chapter (pages 235–245) to find the details of someone they may feel comfortable with, and share the details so they can decide whether or not to engage a professional. If you both feel comfortable, it could be nice for you to go with your loved one to their appointment as extra support (you don't need to go in the room, just be there before and after).

Your loved one may not yet be ready to consider therapy, or maybe they are already in therapy and simply need additional support when in crisis. If this is the case, share the number for Lifeline (13 11 14) with them so you know they have it on hand should they ever need it. You can also phone Lifeline yourself if caring for your loved one becomes overwhelming.

Remember, it is ultimately your loved one's choice whether or not they seek professional support and whether they use that professional support to heal. We are not responsible for their behaviour, but we can support them by providing them with the means to speak with somebody.

Harmful behaviour is not okay, regardless of where it comes from. If you are being harmed by the loved one you are trying to support, or if they are threatening to harm themselves imminently, you are right to immediately call 000.

Before I experienced depression and mental illness so directly, I used to think some people just weren't trying hard enough. Now I think the opposite. I think people with mental illness are the strongest and bravest of us all.

It is so important to understand and acknowledge that your loved one didn't choose to feel this way. It is easy for someone with a sound mind to get frustrated or to feel their loved one is not trying hard enough to get better, or to feel annoyed when they don't put everything they've learned into practice.

When someone is unwell, they don't necessarily have the motivation to get better, and this often means not having the motivation to put into place the tools they've learned to better their mental health.

Kelly, 39
Northern Rivers, New South Wales

Share the list below with someone in your life who is struggling with their mental health. It includes simple activities to help introduce more calm and happiness into their life. Some rows are left blank to add their own activities.

DO MORE	DO LESS
Put my feet in the grass	Listen to crime podcasts
Turn on 'Do Not Disturb' on my phone	Read books that feature plotlines about abuse
Do my Five Joyful Things (see page 211)	Watch the news
Deep breathe with eyes closed	Scroll social media without purpose
Light the good candle (instead of saving it for a rainy day)	Consume too much caffeine
Listen to calming music	Retreat and hide from friends/ family
Take my medication/vitamins	Eat junk food
Text friends or meet up with them	Sleep in dirty clothes or sheets

When holding space for someone who is having trouble with their mental health, it can sometimes have a harmful impact on us. We all know the guidance we receive from flight attendants before flying – that we must fit our own emergency masks before helping another person. This is a good analogy to remember when supporting someone we love who is suffering. Taking care of ourselves in tandem with taking care of them is important.

No matter how much we love someone, trying to hold them above water can tire us out. So that we can continue to support our loved ones productively, it's important that we check in with ourselves while we're also checking in with them.

It requires a lot of someone to be a support person. It requires constant learning, trying and failing and trying again. It requires you to really check in on yourself and to set boundaries – which is hard when all you want to do is help someone. It requires you to continually learn. It requires you to read books, to listen to podcasts, to speak with your loved one and other specialists who might be able to help, to help them with nutrition, exercise and sleep, to see a therapist of your own.

Kelly, 39
Northern Rivers, New South Wales

Checking in with ourselves

After we've finished talking to a loved one in crisis, we can head to a quiet room and ask ourselves:

- Am I feeling okay? Am I overwhelmed or do I feel like I still have some energy in the tank?
- While I'm supporting the person I love, who is supporting me? Does my partner or my own therapist need to be aware of my support, so I can lean on them?

- Can I realistically do this now, or do I need to set a boundary and protect myself by referring my friend or family member to somebody else who can help them?
- Am I able to continue my everyday activities, such as work and family commitments, while supporting my loved one? If these activities are being impacted, how long can this continue for?
- What have I done for my own mental wellbeing lately? What can I easily do to create a 'third space' and separate my support from other moments of my day?
- Is there another way I can support my loved one that may not be as emotionally draining? For instance, could I offer to clean their room, take them for a nice drive, drop over some pre-cooked and nourishing meals?

Remember, we should give only what we can. Even a little support can make a big difference.

Chapter 16

If you only read one chapter . . .

Your top ten takeaways

Congratulations on making it this far in *Paperback Therapy*! It shows a real commitment to doing the work, and bettering yourself and your mental health. Well done. Don't forget to celebrate your progress and reward yourself for sticking with it.

You've no doubt learned a lot about yourself and therapy through reading this book. I hope you've highlighted and dog-eared sections that you wish to revisit or share with loved ones at a later date.

To make it easy for you, below are ten important takeaways from *Paperback Therapy*, written as affirmations. Why not write out your favourite one and stick it on your wall, encouraging you to always put yourself and your mental health first?

1. **Talking about therapy is good.** People from all walks of life benefit from seeing a therapist, although not everyone can access professional support. Some people have a regular therapist they see once a week; others have someone they check in with when life feels a little too tough; and many are considering therapy but haven't found the right person, or the means to afford it yet. There is nothing wrong

with seeing a therapist, or telling those in our lives that we have a therapist supporting us, or simply talking about our mental health with a trusted confidant (if that's what we choose to do). In fact, doing so shows we're invested in becoming the best and happiest person we can be. The more we talk about this as a society, the better we'll all be.

2. Everybody has ups and downs. Life will never be all sunshine and rainbows. Bad days can happen because of something out of our control like loss or grief, our hormones (especially if we're born female), what someone else says to us, an unexpected bad result on a test, an illness and even the weather. It's okay if we sometimes need a little support to get through the low points in life, whether that be from our friends, family, a therapist or even quality time with our pet. Just believe that this is temporary, and the high points will come back around soon. Remember too that no one has it all figured out; happiness comes from first accepting this.

3. I am not my thoughts. Intrusive thoughts have a way of popping into our heads when we least expect them. That doesn't mean that they are real. Remember, we all have thoughts that are scary or a little uncomfortable, but we don't need to act on them. When we have an intrusive thought that makes us feel yucky, we can bring ourselves back to the present and do some exercises to help separate fact from feelings. There is no such thing as a permanent state of mind, and remembering that 'this too shall pass' can help us push through the harder moments.

4. Happiness comes from being engaged with life. Research shows that people who engage with their community through social pursuits are happier than those who don't.[1] With work, school, family commitments and other outside triggers taking up a lot of our time, sometimes this type of active involvement can seem like just another thing to add to the to-do list. The best way we can get

over this way of thinking is to make connection a habit that we enjoy, finding a way to engage with life that offers us a tangible reward that we can see and that gives us a sense of achievement. This could be caring for a pet and taking it for walks, planting and tending to a vegetable patch, volunteering at your local op shop or school canteen, actively participating in your friendships by asking your mates to join you on errands such as grocery shopping, reading a book outside, or making something with your hands and without a screen (building a cubbyhouse, fixing up a car or motorcycle, completing a paint-by-numbers or a puzzle). The opportunities to engage with life are endless – what could you do today to spark a little happiness?

5. I will continue to check in on myself. As per the second takeaway, life will not always be smooth sailing. Sometimes we may feel fantastic after a solid few months of 'doing the work', and then all of a sudden we feel a little flat. When this happens, we must remember to check in on ourselves and ask whether we are following all the tips and tricks we've learned to regulate our emotions, tap into happiness and live by our values. If you like resolutions and goals, setting a monthly reminder to check in on yourself on the first of each month can ensure this important act becomes a ritual. Why not set some diary alerts right now?

6. I will focus on what I can control. Outside triggers have the ability to impact our mood if we let them. It's easy to dismiss negative outside triggers when we know we can't control them, and instead shift our focus to what we can control. When something is bugging you, draw one circle (about the size of the base of a coffee cup) inside an even bigger circle (or even better, copy the template from page 25). In the smaller circle, write down what you can control. Some examples may be: 'My reaction', 'Who I spend time with', 'What time I go to sleep', 'How much I check my phone', etc. In the bigger circle, write down what is out of your control. Some examples may be: 'What people say about me', 'Other people's social posts',

'The weather', etc. Now, shift your focus to the inner circle – the less you ruminate on the things outside of your control (the outer circle), the less important they will seem. Try not to worry about the uncertainty of life – it's one of the best parts! Take one step, one moment at a time, and break up your big goals into little ones to prevent the overwhelm (and feeling of loss of control).

7. My priority is mental wellbeing. Taking away everything else, what is your number one, overarching priority? If it's to be happy and content with life, then the goal is to make your mental well-being the best it can be. Anything that does not help us to reach this goal should take a back seat. To get into the habit of prioritis-ing our mental wellbeing, any time we are about to do, say, buy or try something, we should ask ourselves, 'Does this support the life I'm trying to create?' If the answer is 'no', or it feels slightly off in our tummy, then we need to reconsider our actions. By practis-ing this constantly, prioritising our mental wellbeing will become second nature – and we'll feel the benefits across most areas of our lives.

8. I will trust my gut. A 'gut feeling' often comes up when a decision has to be made. It's an intuitive feeling that is actually based in neuroscience.[2] You see, to trust our gut is to trust our instincts – that internal compass that helps us tell right from wrong. When talking about mental wellbeing, 'gut feelings' can help us process information and make a decision. Importantly, we don't only feel gut feelings in the tummy. When things feel 'off', they may manifest through a prickling sensation in our body, sweaty palms, 'butter-flies' or nausea in our stomach, or tension in our shoulders and jaw. When our 'gut feeling' is positive, we may have a moment of clarity, feel ourselves exhaling deeply after seemingly holding our breath for a long time, or feel a wave of calm come over us after we've made a decision. Learning to pay attention to our mind–body connection is a great therapeutic tool.

9. **I am lovable.** Everybody is worthy of being loved, and you are no exception. You may be a great friend to others, a star player on your basketball team, an important contributor at work. But being lovable isn't really about our talents and good qualities – being lovable is inherent, it is not something we should feel we have to earn, or that is dependent on others. We may doubt how lovable we are due to experiences from our childhood that have left us with self-doubt, or experiences in later life that shake our self-confidence. But learning to love ourselves – including by working on our self-esteem using the tips in this book – can help us to become more confident and mentally strong.

10. **I will find the right therapist for me.** Finding the right therapist takes time. We may cycle through nine different therapists before we find the one who is a good fit. That is okay, because the right therapist is the one who we will build a good rapport with and who we are excited to share our feelings with, knowing they can support us to better wellbeing. It is okay to 'break up' with our therapist if they're not quite right, and to ask friends or Google how to find a better-suited practitioner to support us (see the next chapter for some tips). It's also okay to ask for support from those we trust if we don't have the means to see a therapist right now. Talking about our mental health is much better than keeping discomfort bottled up inside.

Now you know the top ten tips to practise to become a happier, healthier you. How do you feel?

Chapter 17

Seeking professional help

How to find a therapist

Now you've got a taste of what therapy can do to protect and nourish your mental health, you may wish to seek professional help from a qualified therapist in your area for a deeper, more personalised approach. Working with therapists gives us access to tailored professional guidance that can help us get unstuck from our mental hang-ups by identifying, challenging and working through our unhelpful thoughts, feelings and behaviours.

But where do we even begin when seeking professional help? Below are some tips to help you if you're looking to engage a personal therapist.

Starting the search

There are several great resources for finding therapists in Australia. These three are a great place to start:

- **Search engines**: Good old Google works perfectly well for finding a therapist near you. Type in 'counsellor near me' or 'therapist near me' to start wide, adding additional search terms (e.g. 'female', 'Lebanese', 'Christian', 'LGBTQIA+') depending on your specific wants, to find someone who is like-minded. Note that fees, gender and payment options are not always listed on a therapist's own website. This is where reaching out with an enquiry plays an important role (see the next section for more on this).

- **Psychology Today (psychologytoday.com/au)**: Housing an online database of vetted therapists in Australia and around the world, the Psychology Today website allows you to filter by search terms such as location, areas of interests or specialty issues (depression, anxiety, addiction, etc.), payment options (including health insurance), type of therapy practised (art therapy, CBT, ACT, etc.), the therapist's gender, the therapist's age, the price per session and more. In addition to being a database for therapists around the world, the Psychology Today website also has a great back catalogue of articles from the print magazine of the same name, written by experts in specific fields of therapy across topics including relationships, motivation, memory, burnout and more.

- **Friends and family**: It's a little unorthodox – particularly if you're not used to talking about your feelings or mental health with those closest to you – but if your friend recommends a therapist, and you get along with that friend, then it's likely you'll also get along with their therapist. Worried they'll spill about your session? A therapist is ethically mandated by their governing body to not disclose anything from your session to anyone else. It is best to disclose if you were referred to the therapist by someone they are already seeing or have seen, so the therapist can decide if they – and you – will be comfortable. If either of you aren't comfortable, they will have a network of like-minded colleagues who you could be referred to.

You can use the above methods to find a therapist that best suits your needs. It helps to consider what these needs may be before doing your search. Perhaps you want a therapist who identifies as the same gender as you, or who is closer to your place of work so you can visit for a session on the way home, who comes from your culture so they understand your unique nuances, or who specialises in your area of concern (body image, stress, relationships, etc.). After using filters and search terms to narrow down your options, it's a simple web form, email or phone call to find out more information and check if they may have availability to see a new client.

Enquiring if a therapist is available

As therapists see clients regularly and often, many are not able to take on new clients. You may need to reach out to several of the therapists on your shortlist to find one who a) suits your needs, and b) has a free appointment time to book a session with you.

Here is a great email template to use when reaching out to see if therapists have availability.

Hi Tammi,	← Say hi!
I am seeking support for extreme feelings of stress. I have been unable to cope at work and cry at the littlest thing.	← List your reasons for seeking help. This helps your therapist decide if they can help you.
Do you currently have availability for new clients? I live in Smithson and am available to see you Wednesdays between 2 and 5 pm, or Fridays between 10 am and 1 pm.	← Let your therapist know you are local to their office and when you may be free to visit them, so they can see if these session timeslots are currently available in their schedule.
Alternatively, I am open to telehealth sessions if the above appointment times are not available.	← Note whether you would be happy to do telehealth calls, as these are also an option for some therapists.
You can reach me on 0412 345 678 or you can reply by email.	← Give two methods of contact. Sometimes a therapist will email, call or even text in between sessions.
Thank you, *Jane Smith*	← Say goodbye!

If a therapist does not have availability to see new clients, they will often refer you to another therapist in their network or area whom they recommend.

Deciding which therapist is right for you

Finding the right therapist doesn't always happen with the first try. When I first set out on my own search for a therapist, it took me a while to find someone who was the right fit. I've had male therapists make my female-centric problems feel invalid, I've had difficulty seeing therapists in fancy offices when I wanted to talk about status anxiety, and I've had therapists charge exorbitant fees that I simply couldn't maintain at that point in my life. Keeping your own needs in mind when searching for and reaching out to potential therapists can help avoid mismatches.

Compliance and consistency are the best ways to assure success in any wellness journey – whether it is exercise, eating well, or therapy. This means going regularly, complying with a set schedule and 'doing the work'. And you're not going to want to do any of this if your therapist isn't a good fit!

The most important thing when deciding to say 'Yes' to the therapist is that *you* feel comfortable. Most therapists offer a 'sense-check' session to see if you both feel good about the partnership. This is often a no-charge, obligation-free, 10–15-minute phone call where they tell you a little bit about their therapy (the style of therapy they use, how long they've been practising, client types and issues they specialise in, etc.), and you tell them a little about yourself and your reasons for seeking support. After asking some questions, you are free to make a decision about whether you want to book in your first session, if you'd prefer to think about it and book at a later date, or if you're not going to book in with them at all.

If it's the latter and you just didn't vibe with the first therapist you had an exploratory phone call with, please don't let that stop your search. There are so many fantastic therapists out there – you will find one that works for you, promise!

Questions to ask your therapist

Fifteen minutes sounds like a long time when you're chatting to someone casually, but actually it can go by very fast. Having a list of questions that you want to ask your potential therapist in the exploratory phone call will help to keep you – and them – on track, and ensure you can make an informed decision once you hang up the phone.

Here are some example questions and why you should ask them.

What days and times do you practise?	←	Work out whether their availability matches your own.
Do you offer telehealth as well as in-person sessions?	←	If you are unwell and cannot attend in person, it is good to know that there is another option. Many therapists began offering telehealth in 2020 and continue to do so.
Do you go to therapy yourself?	←	While not a deal-breaker, a therapist who goes to therapy is committed to doing the work themselves – always a good sign.
What kind of training did you do?	←	This helps you understand if they have experience in the areas they claim to specialise in, and if they are up to date with the latest skills.
		Note that most industry organisations have continuing professional development (CPD) requirements to ensure members are always learning.
What modalities do you practise?	←	Find out about the type of therapy and activities you may be in for if you work with them.

What organisations
are you a member of?   ←   Australian therapists should be a member of an industry organisation, which helps to track their CPD and supervision (kind of like mentoring) hours. Organisations include the Psychotherapy and Counselling Federation of Australia (PACFA), Australian Counselling Association (ACA), Australian Psychological Society (APS), Australian Psychology Accreditation Council (APAC) and more.

Your therapist may also be part of an organisation related to their specialty area of practice.

Are you LGBTQIA+/
Christian/
Blak- friendly?   ←   While the job of the therapist is to be judgement free and to welcome all clients with unconditional positive regard, you may feel more comfortable if they share the same values or cultural background as you. Asking this question can ensure you feel safe to open up about what's concerning you.

What are your fees
and cancellation
policy?   ←   Therapists are in demand, so it is important they have set fees and a cancellation policy in order to make the most of their time. Ask your therapist what their fees and cancellation policy are, so that you can be sure they are a sustainable option for you.

An example of a cancellation policy is: 50 per cent of the fee if you cancel within forty-eight hours, and 100 per cent of the fee if you cancel less than forty-eight hours before your session, or if you are a no-show or more than ten minutes late to your session.

How do you store your client records?   ←

The information you reveal in therapy is often very sensitive. Therapists take notes to ensure they can pick up where you left off in the previous session, and track patterns in thoughts, feelings and behaviour so you can do better work in the long term. As a result, you have a right to know how client data is managed.

Locked filing cabinets, digitally encrypted files and secure servers are all generally safe areas to store client records. However, it is up to you whether you feel comfortable with a therapist's answer to this question.

How will I know if we're a good fit? How will you know if we're making progress together?   ←

Asking these questions enables the therapist to discuss with you how they track progress. They may say they like to regularly check in with their clients to see that they're comfortable with the progression, or they may give you a confidential (name changed) recount of an instance where they didn't 'gel' with a previous client and so they mutually ended the partnership.

Whatever your therapist answers here, be sure to ask yourself the same question: how will you track if they're a good fit and you're getting your money's worth from your sessions?

Breaking up with your therapist

Just as it's okay to not move ahead with booking a session following an exploratory phone consultation, it's also okay to change your regular therapist if you feel they are no longer serving you.

Therapy sessions are personal, and you may feel you have a special relationship with your therapist and that they'll take it personally if you 'break up' with them by asking to discontinue the relationship. Keep in mind that your therapist is a professional, and if they've been practising for some time then you're likely not the first client to decide to stop seeing them. A therapist's preference will always be that their client is engaged in the work, so if you're no longer feeling it, they'll likely be happy to let you find someone else who can support you better.

Should you just ghost them and not book in your next session? No. Just as you are trying to get better at doing things, so too is your therapist. Ending the therapeutic relationship via email, phone call or even at the end of your final session affords them the opportunity to ask why and improve their work for future clients. Of course, you absolutely don't owe your therapist this opportunity – but they sure will appreciate it.

A lot of my friends don't have the money or time to go seek help from a professional to talk about their mental health. A lot of friends also don't have the parental support to get help, and they think their mental health issues aren't as bad as they truly are, such as anxiety and depression. Seeing a therapist would be a great first step.

Jane, 24
Perth, Western Australia

Funding therapy

Therapy can be expensive (that's why you have this book in your hands!) but it is a worthwhile investment in *you*. To get your mind around the cost of therapy, think of it like going to the gym, brushing your teeth, going out with your friends, or eating nourishing foods – therapy is a habit that helps you to be your best self and, ultimately, happier.

That being said, there are a few ways you can fund therapy sessions to make them a bit more manageable. Here are some tips.

- Consider if you need weekly sessions, or if you can draw these out to fortnightly or even once per month. Sometimes, in times of crisis, you might need more regular sessions, but it's totally fine to tell your therapist when you want to switch your schedule and have more time between sessions.
- Visit your GP for a Mental Health Treatment Plan. This is a support plan for a person going through mental health struggles. When you visit your doctor, they will ask you to complete a questionnaire noting how you have felt over the past several days. If they then agree that you need additional support, your doctor will co-create a Mental Health Treatment Plan with you, often including a referral to a psychologist. This plan lets you claim part of the fees for up to ten sessions with a mental health professional each calendar year.[1]
- Use support offered through your school, university, workplace or community.
  - Many high schools have counsellors, chaplains or psychologists on their staff who can offer support by way of a safe place to talk, right through to referring you and/or your family to external professionals.
  - Similarly, many universities offer free therapy sessions to students or discounted sessions to alumni – search the university website or speak to your student representative council to find out more.
  - An Employee Assistance Program (EAP) is a voluntary and confidential service that many businesses have to assist staff

with workplace and/or personal issues that may impact work performance. Check with the HR team or manager to see if your workplace has an EAP.

– Community groups sometimes provide mental health support through education and/or resources, particularly for their more vulnerable members. See below for a list of support resources to access in your community.

Free support resources for communities in Australia

If you are a member of an Aboriginal or Torres Strait Islander community, a culturally and linguistically diverse community or the LGBTQIA+ community, you may be able to access free support services and resources using the following websites:

- Aboriginal and Torres Strait Islander communities: www.headspace.org.au/yarn-safe
- CALD communities: www.embracementalhealth.org.au
- LGBTQIA+ communities: www.queerspace.org.au.

Crisis support lines in Australia

If you are ever in need of immediate assistance or crisis support, please contact the following services, and let your mental health buddy know (see page 221 for more on mental health buddies). In an emergency, please contact 000.

24/7 SUPPORT SERVICES	NON-24/7 SUPPORT SERVICES
Depression and suicide prevention Beyond Blue: 1300 224 636 Lifeline: 13 11 14 Suicide Call Back Service: 1300 659 467 **Children** Kids Helpline: 1800 55 1800 **Aboriginal and Torres Strait Islanders** 13YARN: 13 92 76 **Aboriginal and Torres Strait Islander men** Brother to Brother: 1800 435 799 **Veterans and families** Open Arms: 1800 011 046 **Substance use disorders** National Alcohol and Other Drug Hotline: 1800 250 015	**Eating disorders** Butterfly Foundation: 1800 33 4673 **LGBTQIA+** QLife: 1800 184 527 **Young people** Headspace: 1800 650 890 ReachOut: reachout.com **Male-focused** MensLine Australia: 1300 78 99 78 **Mood disorders** MindSpot: 1800 61 44 34 **Complex mental health** SANE Australia: 1800 18 7263 **Loneliness** FriendLine: 1800 424 287 **Pregnancy and postnatal depression** PANDA: 1300 726 306 **Sexual health** Sexual Health Quarters: (08) 9228 3693

Note: Information correct at time of printing. Google 'mental health crisis support' or call 000 if the above are unavailable.

A safe space for your thoughts

The mind is a beautiful thing. Writing down your thoughts can reveal what you care about and what you hope for. It can even help you put your plans and ideas into action.

But sometimes thoughts can be overwhelming. When we focus on negative thoughts repetitively, they can begin to feel 'true' or 'real' even when that may not be the case. You can stop the cycle of intrusive thoughts before they become harmful by getting them out of your head and onto the page, where you can make sense of them from a different perspective.

Use these pages to jot down your own thoughts, make lists and draft doodles as you work your way through *Paperback Therapy*. You never know what trends and patterns you may find.

Notes

_____

_____

_____

_____

_____

_____

_____

_____

_____

_____

_____

RATE YOUR SELF-ESTEEM:

Notes

_____

_____

_____

_____

_____

_____

_____

_____

_____

_____

_____

_____

RATE YOUR SELF-ESTEEM:

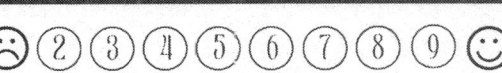

Notes

_____

_____

_____

_____

_____

_____

_____

_____

_____

_____

RATE YOUR SELF-ESTEEM:

☹ ② ③ ④ ⑤ ⑥ ⑦ ⑧ ⑨ ☺

Notes

_____

_____

_____

_____

_____

_____

_____

_____

_____

_____

_____

RATE YOUR SELF-ESTEEM:

☹   ☺

Notes

_____

_____

_____

_____

_____

_____

_____

_____

_____

_____

_____

RATE YOUR SELF-ESTEEM:

☹ ② ③ ④ ⑤ ⑥ ⑦ ⑧ ⑨ ☺

Notes

_____

_____

_____

_____

_____

_____

_____

_____

_____

_____

_____

_____

RATE YOUR SELF-ESTEEM:

Notes

RATE YOUR SELF-ESTEEM:

 ② ③ ④ ⑤

Notes

_____

_____

_____

_____

_____

_____

_____

_____

_____

_____

RATE YOUR SELF-ESTEEM:

     6 7 8

Notes

_____

_____

_____

_____

_____

_____

_____

_____

_____

_____

_____

RATE YOUR SELF-ESTEEM:

         ☺

Notes

_____

_____

_____

_____

_____

_____

_____

_____

_____

_____

_____

RATE YOUR SELF-ESTEEM:

     ⑥   ☺

Notes

_____

_____

_____

_____

_____

_____

_____

_____

_____

_____

_____

RATE YOUR SELF-ESTEEM:

  ③ ④

Glossary

Improve your health literacy with this list of common therapy terms

Abuse: The cruel and violent treatment of a person physically, mentally or emotionally; **of substances**: The improper use of something, such as drugs or alcohol. Also known as **use**.

Addiction: The condition of taking harmful substances (drugs, alcohol) and being unable to stop taking them.

Ambivalence: Presence of two opposing ideas, attitudes or emotions within a person that decreases their readiness to change.

Anxiety: A chronic, complex emotional state, with apprehension or dread as its most prominent component; characteristic of various nervous and mental disorders.

Behaviour: The way a person or animal acts.

Beliefs: Ideas that a person accepts as truth.

Blocks: Internal emotional and psychological constraints that prevent a person seeking help from moving forward.

Boundaries: Defined rules or limits that a person establishes to protect their security and wellbeing around others.

Burnout: A state of complete mental, physical and emotional exhaustion, usually due to overwork.

Client: A person who seeks support from a therapist. Previously known as a **patient**.

Cognition: The mental action or process of acquiring knowledge and understanding through thought, experience and the senses.

Comparisonitis: The compulsion to compare one's accomplishments to another's.

Confidentiality: Responsibility of a therapist to keep personal information of a client private.

Congruent: Genuine, integrated and whole as a person. Opposite of **incongruent**.

Counselling: The provision of professional assistance and guidance in resolving personal or psychological problems.

Countertransferance: A therapist's emotional reactions and projections towards a client, often influenced by their own experiences.

Culture: Distinct collections of attitudes, customs, beliefs and behaviours of a particular group of people.

Depression: A mood disorder that causes a persistent feeling of sadness and loss of interest. Also known as **major depressive disorder**.

Diagnostic and Statistical Manual of Mental Disorders: A handbook used by healthcare professionals as the authoritative guide to the diagnosis of mental disorders. Also known as **DSM-5-TR**.

Echo chamber: An environment where a person only encounters information or opinions that reflect and reinforce their own.

Emotion: A conscious mental reaction subjectively experienced as a strong feeling, usually directed towards a specific object; typically accompanied by physiological and behavioural changes in the body.

Emotional regulation: The complex internal process of modulating emotional arousal, involving the ability to identify, understand and balance one's own emotions in order to function, meet goals and enhance relationships.

Empathy: The ability to understand and share the feelings of another person.

Externalise: To give external existence or form to an emotion or problem. Commonly used in **narrative therapy**.

Feelings: Emotional states or reactions.

Flow: Being 'in the zone', a mental state where a person is fully immersed in a feeling of energised focus, full involvement and enjoyment in the process of an activity.

Grief: Intense sorrow, especially caused by a person's death or other loss.

Health literacy: The access, understanding and use of health information to benefit a person's own health.

Hedonic treadmill: The psychological term for a person's tendency to never truly be happy with their success, pursuing one pleasure after another and pushing out what 'happy' represents.

Hormone: A regulatory substance produced in an organism and transported in tissue fluids such as blood to stimulate specific cells or tissues into action.

Informed consent: The process of agreeing to engage in the process of therapy with full knowledge of the advantages and possible consequences of doing so.

Integrated: A therapy approach that involves integrating skills from different therapeutic sources.

Interpersonal: Relating to relationships or communication between people.

Kessler Psychological Distress Scale: A simple measure of psychological distress. Also known as **K10**.

Meaning making: The act or process of understanding how one exists in and relates to the world.

Mental: Relating to the mind and disorders of the mind.

Mental disorder: A clinically significant disturbance in a person's cognition, emotional regulation or behaviour.

Mental health: A person's condition with regard to their psychological and emotional wellbeing.

Mental Health Treatment Plan: A plan for a person with a mental health disorder, created by a doctor, that outlines the goals for treatment. Also known as a **mental healthcare plan**.

Mental illness: A condition that causes serious disorder in a person's behaviour or thinking.

Mental wellness: A feeling of being balanced, connected to others and ready to meet life's challenges.

Mindfulness: The mental state achieved by focusing awareness on the present moment while calmly acknowledging and accepting feelings, thoughts and bodily sensations.

Mood disorder: A disorder in which the general emotional state or mood is distorted or inconsistent with a person's circumstances and interferes with their ability to function.

Motivational interviewing: A therapy approach drawing on principles and strategies from person-centred therapy and cognitive behaviour therapy, with the aim of increasing a person's motivation to change.

Narrative: A story filled with personal meaning that a person tells about themselves and others.

Person-centred: An approach developed by Carl Rogers whereby emphasis is put on the therapeutic relationship and on reflecting back to the client what they have said.

Physical: Relating to the body as opposed to the mind; relating to things tangibly perceived through the senses.

Post-traumatic stress: Emotional and psychological after-effects of a severe crisis.

Practitioner: A person actively engaged in the profession of therapy; an alternate term for **professional**.

Presenting problem: The initial reason a person seeks help from a therapist.

Psychiatry: The branch of medicine concerned with the study, diagnosis and treatment of mental illness.

Psychology: The scientific study of the human mind and its functions, especially those affecting behaviour in a given context.

Psychotherapy: The treatment of disorders by psychological methods.

Rapport: A close and harmonious relationship in which the people or groups concerned understand each other's feelings or ideas and communicate well.

Reframing: A skill to encourage change in the way a person perceives events or situations.

Schema: A mental codification of experience that includes a particular organised way of perceiving cognitively and responding to a complex situation or set of stimuli.

Selective serotonin reuptake inhibitor (SSRI): A common anti-depressant drug that inhibits the reabsorption of serotonin by neurons, increasing the availability of serotonin as a neurotransmitter.

Self: A person's essential being that distinguishes them from others, especially when considered as part of introspection through therapy.

Self-esteem: A person's confidence in their own worth or abilities.

Session: The interaction of the client and therapist, performed individually or in a group setting.

Shadow work: The process of becoming conscious of an aspect of one's own subconscious.

Society: A group of people who live together in a particular social system, or who are considered as a group.

Socratic questioning: Disciplined and thoughtful dialogue between two or more people.

Somatic: Relating to the body, as distinct from the mind.

Stigma: A mark of disgrace associated with a particular circumstance, quality or person.

Substances: Illegal, prescription or over-the-counter drugs, and alcohol.

Substance use disorder: A disorder where a person partakes in uncontrolled use of substances despite harmful consequences.

Suicide: The act of taking one's own life.

Talk therapy: The treatment of mental, emotional, personality and behavioural disorders using methods such as discussion, listening and counselling.

Therapy: The treatment of mental conditions through verbal communication and interaction.

Thought: An idea or opinion produced by thinking, or occurring suddenly in the mind.

Transference: The process in which the client behaves towards their therapist as though the therapist is a significant person from their past, usually a parent.

Trauma: A deeply distressing or disturbing experience; the lasting emotional response that often results from a person living through a distressing event.

Trigger: The cause of an emotional response, usually external to the self.

Values: Principles or standards of behaviour that a person judges as important in life, which guide decision making and behaviour.

Wellbeing: The state of being comfortable, healthy or happy.

Window of tolerance: A zone where a person is best able to thrive, despite external situations.

Acknowledgements

This book was written after one too many conversations with clients, friends and colleagues about the financial and emotional cost of taking care of our mental health. It is written for each of those individuals, and also for you, the reader. I hope it helps, even if in the smallest way.

Thank you to everyone who felt supported enough to share their lived experiences with me as clients or contributors. I hope I have done you justice.

To the experts who contributed to this book and to my peer practitioners (especially the SHRNKS crew and team at Oakdene House Foundation), thank you for the work you do in your respective fields of mental health. The world needs more people like you.

Dr Sarah Ayoub, my dear friend. The idea for *Paperback Therapy* was sparked because you pushed and inspired me. It grew into a fire through our many WhatsApp voice notes. You are my greatest champion and I cannot thank you enough for all you've taught me.

PB, you sent the email that started this whole journey. It happened so fast, and I have you to thank for the introduction that made my dream come true. A thousand times, thank you.

Kirst, from 'Reading Between The Wines' to your BTS knowledge of the industry, you've been my publishing oracle since we were fatefully seated next to one another in 2012. Thank you for everything.

To Emma Nolan, Lizzie King, Polly Simons, Kelly Jenkins, Anna O'Grady and the entire Simon & Schuster Australia team, thank you for your guidance on bringing this resource to life for me and for the readers. Thanks, too, to my copyeditor Emma Driver and cover designer Alissa Dinallo. We've done a great thing, and I'm so pleased to have you on my team.

Thank you to all those friends whose informal chats informed the 'why' of this book. Allan, Andie, Caris, Christie-Lee, Em, Fro, Jayde, Jess, Kate, KC, Lex, Mandy, Matty, Mel, Portch, Sash, Sar, Sazzle, Siobhan, my pod Sophs, Sumshine, Tazzie, Tom and more. I am so grateful you are in my life.

To Ags, Mike, and all the DECstars for your support. I do not take for granted the space you've afforded me so I could create *BARE* and this book. I am so lucky to have found a home at 10 Bond Street with you. Now, let's celebrate!

To my family – immediate and extended, thank you for shaping me into who I am.

Special shout out to Tara and Mel, and my own therapist, MJ. Your advice, guidance and therapeutic wisdom continues to help me grow as a professional, and I don't know how I could ever repay you for all you've shared over the years. The industry is so lucky to have you.

Thank you to those who first gave me – and your Australian audiences – the space to explore mental wellbeing through words, especially Amanda, Valentina, Sangeeta, Nick and Scott.

I cannot write a book about mental health without acknowledging the experience of the First Nations community, especially the Dharug people upon whose traditional land this book was written. Aboriginal and Torres Strait Islander peoples experienced significant trauma during colonisation. I pay my respect to their Elders past and present and extend that respect to all Aboriginal and Torres Strait Islander peoples today.

And finally, to my husband Paul, who picked me up the many times I fell down. I love you. Thank you for sacrificing our limited weekends together so I could write this book. You and Zeus are the most joyful of my Five Joyful Things.

Sources

1 The therapist is in

1   *Therapy costs.* (n.d.). Psychotherapy and Counselling Federation of Australia. www.pacfa.org.au/community-resources/therapy-costs; *How much does seeing a psychologist cost?* (2023). Australian Psychological Society. psychology.org.au/psychology/about-psychology/what-it-costs

2   *Low cost or free mental health services.* (2022). Healthdirect Australia. www.healthdirect.gov.au/low-cost-or-free-mental-health-services

2 Why do I feel so bad right now?

1   Maslow, A.H. (1954). *Motivation and personality.* Harper & Row Publishers.

2   NSW Health and NSW Department of Customer Service. (2023, July 26). *Long COVID.* NSW Government. www.nsw.gov.au/covid-19/testing-managing/long-covid

3   *Job mobility.* (2023, June 30). Australian Bureau of Statistics. www.abs.gov.au/statistics/labour/jobs/job-mobility/latest-release

4   *Survey results: National study of the impact of climate-fuelled disasters on the mental health of Australians.* (2023, January 19). Climate Council. www.climatecouncil.org.au/resources/survey-results-climate-disasters-mental-health/

5   *Survey results: National study of the impact of climate-fuelled disasters.*

6   *Oxytocin: The love hormone.* (2023, June 13). Harvard Health. www.health.harvard.edu/mind-and-mood/oxytocin-the-love-hormone; Watson, S. (2021, July 20). *Dopamine: The pathway to pleasure.* Harvard Health. www.health.harvard.edu/mind-and-mood/dopamine-the-pathway-to-pleasure

7   Tucker, A., & Sgobba, C. (2021, November 1). *How to find relief if your muscles are sore after a workout.* SELF. www.self.com/story/how-deal-post-workout-muscle-soreness-really-painful

8   Beck, D., & Beck, J. (1987). *The pleasure connection.* Synthesis Press.

3 Dr Google and #trending diagnoses

1   Haltigan, J.D., Pringsheim, T.M., & Rajkumar, G. (2023). Social media as an incubator of personality and behavioral psychopathology: Symptom and disorder authenticity or psychosomatic social contagion? *Comprehensive Psychiatry, 121,* 152362. doi.org/10.1016/j.comppsych.2022.152362

2   Perel, E., & Kellaway, L. (2022, September 3). Love re-imagined: Navigating relationships at home, at work, and beyond [Conference session]. FT Weekend Festival, London. www.youtube.com/watch?v=BjdvwbJyyxo.

3   headspace & Colmar Brunton. (2022). *headspace National Youth Mental Health Survey.* headspace; headspace & Colmar Brunton. (2018). *Headspace National Youth Mental Health Survey.* headspace.headspace.org.au/assets/headspace-National-Youth-Mental-Health-Survey-2018.pdf

4   Stuart, H. (2006). Media portrayal of mental illness and its treatments. *CNS Drugs, 20*(2), 99–106. doi.org/10.2165/00023210-200620020-00002

4 CBT, DBT, ACT . . . WTF?

1   Rogers, C. (1951; 2007). *Client-centered therapy.* Robinson.

2   Gottlieb, L. (2019). *Maybe you should talk to someone: A therapist, her therapist, and our lives revealed.* Houghton Mifflin Harcourt.

3   Mental Health Australia. (2022, May 12). *We must stamp out stigma and discrimination if we are to improve our mental health* [Press release]. mhaustralia.org/media-releases/media-release-we-must-stamp-out-stigma-and-discrimination-if-we-are-improve-our

4   *Mental health care and Medicare.* (2023, June 29). Services Australia. www.servicesaustralia.gov.au/mental-health-care-and-medicare?context=60092

7 Hello, little one

1   Krockow, E.M. (2018, September 7). *How many decisions do we make each day?* Psychology Today. www.psychologytoday.com/au/blog/stretching-theory/201809/how-many-decisions-do-we-make-each-day

2   Bradshaw, J. (1990). *Homecoming: Reclaiming and championing your inner child.* Bantam Books.

3   Berry, W. (2017, February 19). *Raising your inner child.* Psychology Today. www.psychologytoday.com/au/blog/the-second-noble-truth/201702/raising-your-inner-child

8 All the feels
1   Breit, S., Kupferberg, A., Rogler, G., & Hasler, G. (2018). Vagus nerve as modulator of the brain–gut axis in psychiatric and inflammatory disorders. Frontiers in Psychiatry, 9, 44. doi.org/10.3389/fpsyt.2018.00044

9 Meaningful connections
1   Levinger, G. (1980). Toward the analysis of close relationships. *Journal of Experimental Social Psychology*, *16*(6), 510–544. doi.org/10.1016/0022-1031(80)90056-6
2   Kaur, S. (2023, August 21). Posted in my Mazda, hopefully will record in a Urus one day [Instagram post]. *Girls That Invest*. www.instagram.com/p/CwJjN5GoAe7/
3   Otten, C. (2021). *The Sex Ed You Never Had*. Allen & Unwin, p. 235.
4   Brennan, K.A., Clark, C.L., & Shaver, P.R. (1998). 'Self-report measurement of adult attachment: An integrative overview', in J.A. Simpson & W.S. Rholes (Eds.), *Attachment theory and close relationships* (pp. 46–76). The Guilford Press.
5   Couper, E. (2023, July 17). 'Nearly half of Aussies' sex lives impacted by cost of living crisis', *The Australian*. www.theaustralian.com.au/news/latest-news/nearly-half-of-aussies-sex-lives-impacted-by-cost-of-living-crisis/news-story/b8731b89dbcabd54969c14998ea3d1d7
6   Kerr, M., & Bowen, M. (1988). *Family evaluation: An approach based on Bowen theory*. Norton.

10 Protecting yourself
1   Bourne, E.J. (2010). *The anxiety and phobia workbook* (5th ed.). New Harbinger Publications, p. 295.
2   *Use Situation-Behavior-Impact (SBI)^{TM} to understand intent*. (2022, December 14). Center for Creative Leadership. www.ccl.org/articles/leading-effectively-articles/closing-the-gap-between-intent-vs-impact-sbii/

11 Creativity is a wild mind
1   Fancourt, D., & Finn, S. (2019). *What is the evidence on the role of the arts in improving health and well-being? A scoping review*. World Health Organization. apps.who.int/iris/bitstream/handle/10665/329834/9789289054553-eng.pdf
2   Fancourt & Finn, p. 3.
3   Hoicka, E. (2017, January 12). Five ways to make your child a creative genius. *The Conversation*. theconversation.com/five-ways-to-make-your-child-a-creative-genius-71170

4   Kotler, S. (2014, February 25). Flow states and creativity: Can you train people to be more creative? *Psychology Today*. www.psychologytoday. com/us/blog/the-playing-field/201402/flow-states-and-creativity

5   Hannemann, B.T. (2006). Creativity with dementia patients: Can creativity and art stimulate dementia patients positively? *Gerontology, 52* (1), 59–65. doi.org/10.1159/000089827

6   Cohut, M. (2018, February 16). *What are the health benefits of being creative?* Medical News Today. www.medicalnewstoday.com/articles/320947

7   Kaimal, G. (2019). Adaptive Response Theory: An evolutionary framework for clinical research in art therapy. *Art Therapy, 36*(4), 215–219. doi.org/10. 1080/07421656.2019.1667670

8   IBM Global Business Services. (2010). *Capitalizing on complexity: Insights from the global chief executive officer study.* www.ibm.com/downloads/ cas/XAO0ANPL

9   McGorry, P. (2020). *Statement from Prof. Patrick McGorry, Professor of Youth Mental Health at the University of Melbourne and Director of Orygen Youth Health Research Centre. Activate Arts Therapists: Support for Mental Health.* Submission to ACTivate Arts Therapists campaign petition. carlavanlaar.com/wp-content/uploads/2020/08/Prof-Pat-McGorry- statement-120820.pdf.

10   White, M. (2007). *Maps of narrative practice.* W.W. Norton.

12 Just one more time

1   *Substance abuse.* (2023). Healthdirect Australia. www.healthdirect.gov.au/ substance-abuse

2   *Alcohol, tobacco & other drugs in Australia.* (2023, June 30). Australian Institute of Health and Welfare. www.aihw.gov.au/reports/alcohol/alcohol- tobacco-other-drugs-australia/contents/about

3   Haber, P.S., Riordan, B.C., Winter, D.T., et al. (2021). New Australian guidelines for the treatment of alcohol problems: An overview of recom- mendations. *Medical Journal of Australia, 25*(7 Suppl.), S1–S32. doi.org/ 10.5694/mja2.51254

4   *Alcohol Use Disorders Identification Test (AUDIT).* (n.d.). auditscreen.org/; Humeniuk, R., Henry-Edwards, S., Ali, R., et al. (2010). *The Alcohol, Smoking and Substance Involvement Screening Test (ASSIST): Manual for use in primary care.* World Health Organization. apps.who.int/iris/handle/ 10665/44320

13 But what if?

1 *Mental health: Prevalence and impact of mental illness.* (2023). Australian Institute of Health and Welfare. www.aihw.gov.au/mental-health/overview/mental-illness

2 *Generalised anxiety disorder.* (2022). Beyond Blue. https://www.beyond-blue.org.au/mental-health/anxiety/types-of-anxiety/gad

3 Gratz, K.L., Tull, M.T., & Wagner, A.W. (2005). 'Applying DBT mindfulness skills to the treatment of clients with anxiety disorders'. In S.M. Orsillo & L. Roemer (Eds.), *Acceptance- and mindfulness-based approaches to anxiety* (pp. 147–161). Springer.

4 *COVID-19 pandemic triggers 25% increase in prevalence of anxiety and depression worldwide.* (2022, March 2). World Health Organization. www.who.int/news/item/02-03-2022-covid-19-pandemic-triggers-25-increase-in-prevalence-of-anxiety-and-depression-worldwide

5 Australian Institute of Health and Welfare (2021). *Australia's welfare 2021: Data insights.* www.aihw.gov.au/getmedia/ef5c05ee-1e4a-4b72-a2cd-184c2ea5516e/aihw-aus-236.pdf.aspx

6 Wilkins et al., *The Household, Income and Labour Dynamics in Australia Survey.*

7 Oaklander, M. (2016, August 24). Old people are happier than people in their 20s. *Time.* https://time.com/4464811/aging-happiness-stress-anxiety-depression/; Blanchflower, D.G., & Oswald, A.J. (2007). *Is well-being U-shaped over the life cycle?* Working Paper 12935, National Bureau of Economic Research. doi.org/10.3386/w12935

8 Rizmal, Z. (2022, February 20). *Anxiety is rising among Australia's young people, but it's not just due to COVID-19.* ABC News. www.abc.net.au/news/2022-02-20/anxiety-young-people-is-increasing-across-australia-covid/100829836

9 Cheung, A.S., Thrower, E., Zwickl, S., et al. (2021). The health and wellbeing of transgender Australians: A national community survey. *LGBT Health, 8* (1), 42–49. doi.org/10.1089/lgbt.2020.0178

10 Sandberg, S. (2013). *Lean in: Women, work, and the will to lead.* Random House, p. 126.

14 Down, but not out

1 Miller, M. (2022, October 12). WandaVision episode eight's quote about grief has become the show's defining moment. *Esquire.* www.esquire.com/entertainment/tv/a35713623/wandavision-episode-8-grief-quote-explained/

2 *Mental health: Prevalence and impact of mental illness.* (2023). Australian Institute of Health and Welfare. www.aihw.gov.au/mental-health/overview/mental-illness

3 *Anxiety and depression during pregnancy and the postnatal period.* (n.d.). Black Dog Institute. www.blackdoginstitute.org.au/wp-content/uploads/2022/06/Depression-during-pregnancy.pdf

4 Li, Y., Lv, M., Wei, Y., Sun, L., Zhang, J., Zhang, H., & Li, B. (2017). Dietary patterns and depression risk: A meta-analysis. *Psychiatry Research: Neuroimaging, 253,* 373–382. doi.org/10.1016/j.psychres.2017.04.020; Khalid, S., Williams, C. M., & Reynolds, S. (2016). Is there an association between diet and depression in children and adolescents? A systematic review. *British Journal of Nutrition, 116*(12), 2097–2108. doi.org/10.1017/s0007114516004359

5 *Exercise & depression.* (n.d.). Black Dog Institute. www.blackdoginstitute.org.au/wp-content/uploads/2022/06/Exercise-and-depression.pdf

6 Statistics in this section are drawn from *Stats & facts.* (2023). Suicide Prevention Australia. www.suicidepreventionaust.org/news/statsandfacts; and *Suicide & self-harm monitoring data.* (2023). Australian Institute of Health and Welfare. www.aihw.gov.au/suicide-self-harm-monitoring/data/suicide-self-harm-monitoring-data

7 *Stats and Facts: Suicide Prevention Australia.* (2023, February 21). Suicide Prevention Australia. www.suicidepreventionaust.org/news/statsandfacts

8 *Suicide and self-harm monitoring data.* (n.d.). Australian Institute of Health and Welfare. www.aihw.gov.au/suicide-self-harm-monitoring/data/suicide-self-harm-monitoring-data

9 *Suicide and self-harm monitoring data.* Australian Institute of Health and Welfare. www.aihw.gov.au/suicide-self-harm-monitoring/data/suicide-self-harm-monitoring-data

10 *Suicide among young people.* (2023, September 1). Australian Institute of Health and Welfare. www.aihw.gov.au/suicide-self-harm-monitoring/data/populations-age-groups/suicide-among-young-people

16 If you only read one chapter

1 For example, Cummins, R.A., Mead, R., & the Australian Unity–Deakin University Wellbeing Research Partnership. (2021). *The Australian Unity Wellbeing Index 20th anniversary commemorative edition.* Australian Unity and Deakin University. www.acqol.com.au/uploads/surveys/20yr-anniversary-report.pdf;

2 *Gut feelings are real, but should you really 'trust your gut'?* (2021, January 27). Healthline. www.healthline.com/health/mental-health/trust-your-gut

17 Seeking professional help

1 *Mental health care and Medicare.* (2023, June 29). Services Australia. www.servicesaustralia.gov.au/mental-health-care-and-medicare? context=60092

Index

List of exercises

About the Author

© Hugh Stewart

Tammi Miller is a Certified Practising Counsellor based in Sydney, Australia. Through her practice, BARE Therapy, Tammi enables clients to work through their blocks and cultivate better mental and emotional wellbeing. Passionate about improved health literacy and with lived experience in mental health as both a psychotherapist and a client, she manages her own mental health using the same techniques she shares with readers in *Paperback Therapy*.

Follow Tammi on Instagram @bare__therapy